Heaven's Answer for the Home

Heaven's Answer for the Home

by
Lowell Lundstrom

Lowell Lundstrom Ministries, Inc.
Sisseton, South Dakota 57262

Box 4000
Winnipeg, Manitoba
R3C 3W1

Heaven's Answer for the Home

Copyright © 1979
Lowell Lundstrom Ministries, Inc.
Sisseton, South Dakota 57262
ISBN O-938220-16-0

Printed in the USA

Contents

7 Preface

9 **Chapter One**
Heaven's Answer to the
Number-One Family Problem

21 **Chapter Two**
Heaven's Language of Love

29 **Chapter Three**
How We Found Heaven
in Our Home

35 **Chapter Four**
Heaven's Answer for Quarreling

43 **Chapter Five**
Heaven's View of You

51 **Chapter Six**
Heaven's Answer for Healing
in Your Home

61 **Chapter Seven**
Heaven's Way to Change Your Mate

67   **Chapter Eight**
Heaven's Way to Discipline
Your Children

78   **Chapter Nine**
Heaven's Laws for In-Laws

88   **Chapter Ten**
Heaven's Way to Stretch Your Pay

99   **Chapter Eleven**
Heaven's Plan for the Married Man

105   **Chapter Twelve**
Heaven's Wisdom for Married Women

111   **Chapter Thirteen**
How You Can Experience the Ultimate
of the Intimate Side of Marriage

121   **Chapter Fourteen**
Heaven and You Can Make It Through

135   **Chapter Fifteen**
Heaven's Motive for Your Marriage

NOTE: *As you read this book, under-line (using a colored pencil) the part you would like your mate to read. Then let your mate underline the part you should read. Turn about is fair play!*

Preface

Two of the most popular newspaper columnists of our day are Ann Landers and Abigail Van Buren, better known as "Dear Ann" and "Dear Abby." The reason for their popularity is that they offer answers, and very good ones, from a human point of view. I've deeply appreciated what Ann and Abby have had to say, but much of Ann's credibility crumbled when she announced the breakup of her marriage to Jules Lederer. Millions asked, "Ann, if you can't keep it all together, how can we?" Ann herself needed Heaven's answer.

A Christian once said, "Being a martyr—dying—that's easy; it's this *living* business that's tough."

More than one married person has felt that death or divorce would be an easy out, preferable to the tough business of living with some of the problems of marriage.

And yet, these problems can be solved. They fall into basic patterns. Others have solved them and found the happiness they dreamed about when they said, "I do."

Let's back up to the moment at the altar. You and your mate brought certain assets to your marriage. These may have been finances or furniture; but, almost unnoticed, you and your spouse brought something else. I call it your psychological baggage. When that baggage is opened—surprise, surprise!

Because of that psychological baggage, problems are programmed into a marriage. You may have heard the phrase, "Heaven help you!" Understanding the problems and solving them, with Heaven's help, is the subject matter of this book.

—Lowell Lundstrom

CHAPTER ONE

Heaven's Answer to the Number-One Family Problem

For the past few years, my wife and I have been conducting Family Life Seminars. We have discovered the number-one family problem. Listen—the number-one family problem is the need for good communication! It seems that, after getting married, some couples become strangers the second time!

Recently I received several letters confirming this discovery. A lady wrote, "We have been Christians for about ten years, but my husband will not communicate about spiritual matters. I have lost my respect for him. He is a poor disciplinarian of his time, his money and his children."

Another lady wrote, "My husband and I have been married 15 years. We're growing apart instead of closer together. I get turned off because he is so indifferent toward the children and me. He leaves the entire responsibility of rearing them—morally and physically—to me. I'm becoming weak emotionally trying to make all of the family decisions."

It came as a surprise for Connie and me to discover that half of the Christian couples with whom we had contact seldom prayed together! It is clear that this lack of communication with God, which is basic to Christian family communications, is taking its toll.

The interests of today's modern family are fragmented by the forces of our society. Early in the morning the dad leaves for work, going one direction; the children leave for school, going another direction; and the wife leaves for work, going another direction.

Then, in late afternoon, the family returns for dinner and spends the evening around the television set. Finally, after the evening news and a little bit of Johnny Carson's *Tonight Show*, the family stumbles toward the bedrooms to live in loneliness. The next day they continue their separate lives of emptiness.

One lady wrote me awhile ago, "Even when I'm lying in bed with my husband I feel so alone I want to cry."

The gray castle of loneliness is a result of a lack of communication. This bleak structure was not in God's plan when He created marriage. God placed Adam in the midst of Paradise. He had all of the animals surrounding him, but not a single one of those animals could really be an intimate friend. *"God said, It is not good that the man should be alone; I will make him an help meet for him"* (Genesis 2:18).

The first reason given for Eve's creation was so that Adam would not be alone. Paradise was beautiful, but it was a lonely place for Adam without someone to share it with. God sensed his loneliness and created Eve to fill the emptiness in his life.

Carl Malz has written a poem expressing Adam's loneliness:

Adam

O God
Of all completeness,
In all creation
I alone am incomplete.

See the man
That You have formed
In Your perfection,
With one exception...

Alone,
I found within
A haunting cry

That echoed through
The empty chambers of my heart.

Until
From slumber You imposed,
I rose
To find another at my side.
We touched.
The echoes died.

The Bible says, "*And the Lord God caused a deep sleep to fall upon Adam, and he slept: and he took one of his ribs, and closed up the flesh instead thereof; and the rib, which the Lord God had taken from man, made he a woman, and brought her unto the man.*"

Adam must have thought, "This is it!"

He said, "*This is now bone of my bones, and flesh of my flesh: she shall be called Woman, because she was taken out of Man. Therefore shall a man leave his father and his mother, and shall cleave unto his wife: and they shall be one flesh*" (See Genesis 2:21-24, *The Living Bible*).

The Bible says a man should leave his father and mother and cleave unto his wife. That means to leave the in-laws out of the marriage. There will be problems in a marriage if the husband and wife do not really leave their parents. Many marital problems are related to in-laws

12

who try to manipulate individuals according to their own will.

According to Webster's Dictionary, the word "cleave" means "to hold fast to, to cling to, or to be faithful to." As a boy clings to his mother emotionally and spiritually, in his maturity he clings to his wife.

A man cleaves to his wife in the beginning; but, as the years go by, his work, his career, his friends and his own selfish pursuits soon win a greater place in his heart than does his wife. Consequently his wife's affection for him begins to shrivel up, driving him farther and farther away from her.

Sometimes a wife will get so involved with her work and so influenced by those with whom she works that her attitude toward her husband changes noticeably.

I know some men who feel more at home at the office, at a bar, on the golf course or out hunting and fishing, than they do in their own homes! The reason for a man's being ill at ease at home is a lack of communication. Often a wife spends more time with the children than the husband does, and consequently he has a natural feeling of being an outsider when it comes to family affairs.

Sometimes, too, a wife will live in an exciting world of her own—at the office—and will withdraw when she comes home to crying kids and a tired husband.

The question then arises: How can we improve communication within families?

Examine the basis of your relationship

A troubled man came to see me after a weekend Family Life Seminar and shared how he had become involved with pornography. His wife was aware of his problem and had been praying for him. This made it all the worse for him because he knew it was wrong for him to commit mental adultery with the women on the pages of those magazines.

He told me, tearfully, "Lowell, when my wife and I were first married everything was great. Then, somewhere along the way things began to fall apart, and I turned to pornographic magazines to spice up our marriage. After this weekend of hearing what you had to say, I realize that the frustration and lack of fulfillment in our marriage was a result of our lack of communication."

Our lives are hectic, to say the least.

Conducting crusades and rallies, preparing radio and television programs, producing records, writing letters, composing songs, plus rearing a family on the road 300 nights a year—these things combined could create such a pressure cooker atmosphere that our marriage would blow up if we weren't Christians. And being Christians is not enough. Connie and I have had to establish some methods of understanding in our relationship with each other that might help you build your marriage stronger for God.

We certainly would not say our marriage is perfect or ideal because we are still working on it every day. But for what it might be worth, we submit the following:

Realize your relationship together depends on your relationship to God

When you are tuned in to God you will know how to tune in to the needs of your mate! Husband and wife, if you have been having problems relating to each other, have you really been taking time to share with each other? A marriage where the husband and wife are fighting isn't nearly as bad off as the marriage where there is ice-cold silence. At least when a couple is fighting they are communicating what they feel. When silence settles in, there is going to be a build-up of frustrations that will blow that marriage apart.

You must communicate with one another to be happily married

Your communication needs to include several

areas. First, you need spiritual communication. God created man a living soul (*"God formed man of the dust of the ground, and breathed into his nostrils the breath of life; and man became a living soul,"* Genesis 2:7). You are a spirit wrapped in flesh, and the only way you can communicate as a spirit is to have a relationship with God through His Holy Spirit.

If you have left Bible reading, prayer and Christian fellowship out of your marriage, you have been short-changing yourself. You may know each other physically and emotionally, but do you know each other spiritually? You *must* have a relationship with God to be able to sense the spiritual needs of your mate.

Connie and I have been married for over twenty-six years. There have been times when I have felt impressed to say something encouraging to Connie just when she needed it. That prompting didn't come from me—it came from the Lord. There have been times when Connie has done the same thing for me—when she said exactly what I needed to hear from the Lord. She ministered to me! When you are tuned in to God, you will discover how to tune in to the needs of your mate, and you will begin to minister to one another.

God not only tempers your personality by the

Holy Spirit—He *amplifies* your love for each other. Connie and I love each other most when we have prayed. There is something about Connie's personality that becomes so much more appealing to me when I sense the Spirit of God moving in her life. Or—maybe it's me— maybe I become more aware of what God is doing in our lives. I know for certain that prayer makes my personality sweeter and more appealing, so probably Connie feels like sharing more of herself with me. I can't figure it out; all I can say is, it works! The bishop was right—"The family that prays together stays together!"

Spiritual life and marriage are inseparable. The Bible says, *"Here is another thing that you do: you weep and moan, and you drown the altar of the Lord with tears, but he still refuses to look at the offering or receive an acceptable gift from you. You ask why. It is because the Lord has borne witness against you on behalf of the wife of your youth. You have been unfaithful to her, though she is your partner and your wife by solemn covenant. Did not the one God make her, both flesh and spirit? And what does the one God require but godly children? Keep watch on your spirit, and do not be unfaithful to the wife of your youth"* (Malachi 2:13-15, *New English Bible*).

Second, you need to communicate emotionally! When young couples are going together and considering marriage, they talk, talk, talk, talk. They share every emotional experience together. Then the schedules and duties of married life settle down upon them after they're married until they feel uncomfortable sharing the petty problems and frustrations they have encountered during the day.

Sometimes they are too tired to even talk, so each day's frustrations are buried within. Each day you can smell an odor of dissatisfaction in that household, and before long the husband and wife say, "We're unhappy in this marriage. We both want out." The answer is not in getting out. The fact is that the marriage needs an emotional cleansing.

Someone said, "The way a man spells love to his family is T-I-M-E." Husband, take time to hold your wife in your arms. Take time to let her share her problems with you. Wife, take time to hear your husband out. Turn off the television set, give up that plastic, make-believe world you're watching and begin to live your own life. You need to communicate with each other.

Third, you need to communicate socially! Are you friends with your mate? Do you like to go places together? What is your social life like? Some marriages die from boredom. If the husband and wife would remember what they did on dates when they first went together, they could breathe a lot of life back into their relationship. The best way to get an "old flame" burning brightly again is to give it fresh air.

How long has it been since you took your wife out for a date? How long has it been since you let your wife get away from the children for awhile?

Merle Haggard, the popular country-western singing star, had a hit record that described a couple desperately trying to get their marriage moving again. The man says, "Let's go away for a weekend alone, spend some time communicating, and then if we're not back in love by Monday, we'll go our separate ways."

Fourth, you need to communicate physically. By physically I'm not talking about sex alone. I'm talking about the tender touches, the unexpected kisses, holding hands, sitting closely to each other when riding along in the car. These and many other magic moments combine to make a relationship meaningful.

Why do lovers forget the very things that helped them fall in love in the first place? Now, this isn't childish. As I mentioned, the man should cleave to his wife as he once cleaved to his mother. A mother holds her son, she makes a big fuss over him, she touches him, she combs his hair, she helps him. This touching is a tremendous way of communicating feeling.

God wants you to be happy with your mate. If

you're not as happy as you should be, examine your communication.

CHAPTER TWO

Heaven's Language of Love

A survey involving 100,000 couples showed that passionate love lasts an average of two years. If the husband and wife are not good friends at the end of two years, their marriage will die.

Many couples have said they loved each other more when they were dating than after they were married! The reason is that they communicated more on their dates. If you see a couple in a restaurant, nose to nose, smiling and whispering, chances are they are dating. If you see another couple staring blankly at their menus, you can guess they are married.

Communication is the language of love. If you want to improve your relationship—if you want to feel the fire of love burning like it once did—begin by opening your lines of communication. This will take time and understanding.

Remember, communicating is *more* than talking with each other. Communication, in a lover's understanding of the word, begins when you share your inner self in such a way that your mate really gets to know you better.

In his book, *Why am I Afraid to Tell You Who I Am?*, John Powell says that we communicate on five different levels, from the most shallow cliches to open honesty. I am using John's outline to illustrate this truth.

Level five—cliche conversation

To illustrate these five levels, imagine your husband coming home from work. He walks through the door and says, "Nice to see you, honey! Did you have a good day?" You reply, "I guess it was okay." What have you said? Nearly nothing. Your conversation was only an exchange of courtesies.

Level four—reporting the facts about others

Then you say, "Did you hear that Bill has been promoted to district manager of his company and that he and Mary will be moving to Chicago?" Now you have shared an expression of substance; however, you may not be communicating fully about this situation.

Level three—expressing your ideas and judgments

This is revealed when you say, "You know, I don't think Bill and Mary are going to like Chicago. After living all these years in this small town, they are going to get claustrophobia living in the crowded, windy city."

Level two—expressing your feelings and emotions

You would show this by mentioning, "I'm really going to miss Mary. She was the only one I could ever go to when I had a problem with the children. I don't know what I am going to do when she leaves!"

Level one—complete emotional and personal communication

This finally comes out when you tell your husband, "Why can't we talk about our problems? Why do I have to talk to Mary when I feel depressed? Why can't I feel as close to you as to Mary?"

Now you have opened up and begun to communicate your real self. Self-revealing communication is important if you want to maintain the "soul" of your marriage. Otherwise, you are just two personalities bound together by a marriage contract and compelled to live in the same house.

Two things are needed for open communication. First, you need to feel *loved and accepted.* Love frees you to come out of your cocoon. We are all like butterflies trying to emerge from the cocoons of our circumstances. If we cannot emerge, we will die in bondage without having experienced fullness of life. If we are allowed to emerge from the protective barriers we have built around ourselves, we will fly higher than ever before. The most destructive position to be in is to be bound to someone who does not love you, who will not allow you to escape from your limited self.

Second, you need *courage to communicate.* Communicating is a risky business! There is always a chance that someone will misunderstand you. You must express your inner feelings and frustrations, even when they don't make sense to you, in order to keep your relationship growing.

A few months after Connie knew she was expecting a baby, I went through an unusual experience.

It seemed that Satan attacked me with a barrage of doubts about the child's welfare.

Satan told me the child was going to be born retarded. This was a difficult struggle because I have a retarded uncle and Connie has a mongoloid sister. Throughout the years we have felt compassion for retarded children and their parents. My concern wasn't that I could not accept a retarded child, but the thought of traveling with a child with less than normal mental capacity, with the erratic schedules we have to maintain, was very disturbing.

I never mentioned anything to Connie about my inner struggle, but she sensed that something was not right. In fact, at that very time she was under satanic attack with doubts of the same nature.

She didn't want to say what she was feeling and neither did I, but one night she turned to me and said, "Lowell, do you really want this child?" I was shocked at her words, and I determined to share the spiritual struggle I was experiencing.

When I told her how Satan was attacking me with thoughts that the child would be born retarded, she began to cry and shared how she had been having the same struggle. As soon as we shared the conflict, we could see Satan was trying to rob us of the blessing of our new child.

I was in the middle of a crusade in Sterling, Colorado, when Connie called me from Sisseton. Little Lance LaDell was born, normal and healthy!

When I asked her how little Lance compared with the other three children when they were born, she laughed and said, "Lowell, he's the best one of the bunch!"

I thank God we were able to pray together when our relationship came under satanic attack. Think of the millions of couples fighting spiritual battles who cannot share their burdens with the Lord or with each other. In order to keep their marriage going smoothly, the partners need to keep the doors of communication open, vertically to heaven and horizontally to each other.

If you want to improve your use of the language of love with your mate, I suggest you take these following steps:

Be honest with God!

Remember, the Bible says, *"We wrestle not against flesh and blood, but against principalities, against powers, against the rulers of the darkness of this world, against spiritual wickedness in high places"* (Ephesians 6:12). What God has joined together all of hell is going to try to put asunder (See Mark 10:9). You can know for certain that if God is for your marriage, the devil is against it.

Many couples have felt forces driving them apart without realizing they were under satanic siege. The only way to break the powers that divide is to become honest with God.

If you haven't been living for God, if you have neglected to strengthen your relationship by reading the Bible and praying together, if you have allowed the sanctuary of your home to be infiltrated by a steady diet of television which has destroyed your times for sharing with each other—confess your wrongdoing. Ask God to forgive you. God cannot help you until you're honest enough to admit your mistakes and make a real effort to make things right.

Then, *be honest with each other!*

When you are living together as man and wife, you are too close to completely hide your inner feelings from each other. Trying to hide them is just as foolish as the little boy trying to hide his basketball under the covers of his bed. His mother can see the lump. Even though he may deny the fact, the evidence is there.

A poisoned relationship is just like a boil. Sometimes you need to go to the doctor to have it lanced before it will heal. This is why if your marriage is in bad shape I suggest you go to someone you both trust, a marriage counselor or a qualified pastor, so you can get things out into the open to heal.

I have found that men are the most reluctant to go for counseling. A man by nature is proud, and it is difficult for him to admit that his marriage is failing and that he is helpless to save it.

If going to God in repentance or going to a marriage counselor sounds difficult, consider the consequences of your refusal. Your marriage may be destroyed, your children may be scarred for life, and you may end up like a dried larva in a cocoon—unless you are released from your bondage.

Communication is the language of love. If you love God, begin to communicate by saying, "I'm sorry." God will understand. If you want to communicate with your mate, *the same words will work*.

God is for your marriage! He wants it to succeed. Give Him the opportunity to help.

CHAPTER THREE

How We Found Heaven in Our Home

As Connie and I look back on our years of ministry together, we see that God has enabled us to build a relationship together that has become more exciting than ever! Here are some suggestions you may find helpful in your marriage:

We realize our relationship together depends upon our relationship to God and our obedience to His Word

If either of us fails to read God's Word and pray, we can tell it right away in our marriage. There is an unspoken language in every personal relationship between two people. When Connie is uptight or easily irritated, or I find my patience growing short, we realize these are danger signals that tell us we need to get closer to the Lord.

We know that we are married for life

As we look back upon the roughest times in our marriage, when the tension of traveling and ministry wore us down physically and psychologically, when our nerves were frayed to a frazzle—even if we had a bad argument we knew we would stay together because we were married for life. Jesus said, *"What God hath joined together, let no man put asunder"* (Matthew 19:6).

I think one of the worst forces breaking up marriages today is the idea, "If things don't work out, we'll split and go separate ways." Marriage used to be considered a lifetime contract. Today some people think it's a 90-day option!

Recently a friend said, "It's possible to have unison without unity. If you tie two cats together by their tails and hang them over a clothes line you have unison—but you don't have unity." I laughed at the idea, but I realize there are many husbands and wives legally joined together on paper. They are joined emotionally and physically but have never agreed spiritually to make their marriages work regardless of the cost.

If you don't pledge yourself to God and to each other for life, the pressure of your different personalities may drive you apart. A great stabilizing force is the realization that you are married *forever* in the sight of God and divorce is a course of action you will never consider unless there is prolonged unfaithfulness or brutality.

Trust is a great help

Connie and I talked about trust recently, and we discovered that we have never worried about each other's faithfulness once during the years of our relationship. Connie knows I have always been faithful to her—and I know she has always been faithful to me. We never worry about each other when we're apart.

President Jimmy Carter taught an adult Sunday School class at the First Baptist Church in Washington, D.C. He told his class, "Couples should make a lifetime commitment to each other. When fidelity is abused, when a husband or wife succumbs to temptation, that's when faithfulness is paramount."

I appreciated President Jimmy Carter's emphasis on the importance of a lifetime commitment and the need for faithfulness.

Infidelity destroys character. Every man who cheats on his wife destroys something priceless within his own character. Every woman who cheats on her husband has destroyed the beauty of innocence that should radiate from her life.

Sin shows, and the devil knows if he can get someone to cheat, the marriage is weakened.

Sharing has been one of the best tools in our marriage

Connie and I spend a lot of time talking to each other. We like to read books together. During recent years we have read at least twenty different manuals on how to build a happy Christian marriage. Connie underlines the portions she thinks I need to read, and I underline the portions I think she needs to read. Needless to say, our books are really marked up! I suggest you do the same as you read this book.

Communication is the basis of any relationship. If you are having problems in your marriage, you've got to talk things out. The Bible says, *"Don't let the sun go down on your wrath"* (Ephesians 4:26).

One couple was advised, "When you get married, make sure you never go to bed unless all of your arguments are settled." About six months later someone saw the groom and he looked frazzled out. He was asked, "What's the matter with your marriage?" The groom replied, "You told me never to go to bed unless our arguments were settled. I haven't had any sleep for six months!"

If your mate won't talk, talk to him. If your mate won't answer you, write your problems in a letter. There has to be communication or you will never have a happy home.

Most of all, Connie and I have common spiritual values

We are not living together for what we can get out of our marriage. We're not living for ourselves. We're loving and serving the Lord as a team to help others find Jesus Christ. This same motive can be yours whether or not you are in the ministry. Today God is raising millions of lay men and women who are actively sharing Christ with their families and friends.

If your marriage is a selfish affair, if you are trying to get out of it all you can for yourself, you will never be as happy as you could be serving God together.

Happiness is more of a by-product than a destination. If you are not living for God, you are probably living for material things: the house, the car, the boat, the furniture. Material things are big in your brain. Or you might be living for sex. The problem with so many Americans is they are trying to get more out of sex than there is in it. That is why some couples end up trying kinky, weird things and find less satisfaction than ever before. One woman who tried a kinky sex trick said, "I've tried every novelty; normal sex is best."

There are three partners in a Christian marriage

It takes three to make a marriage—a husband, a wife, and God! Connie and I have been fortunate to have God helping us. The Lord is the best marriage counselor in the world. When you come up against a problem in your marriage and there is no way out—God always finds a way. He makes a way. If God doesn't change the problem, He changes you or your attitude toward that problem so you can overcome it.

Connie and I have discovered that the way to have heaven in our home is to have the Christ of heaven in our hearts. It will work for you, too!

CHAPTER FOUR

Heaven's Answer for Quarreling

A friend of mine was called to the home of a young couple who were about to have an explosion—literally! When he walked in the door, the husband said to his mother-in-law with whom he and his wife were living, "The thing that made me angry was that you went and called the cops!"

She replied, "I only did that because you were going to drop a lighted match down the gas tank of my car."

I would say that was an explosive situation!

In this chapter we'll take a look at basic marriage conflicts to see how to avoid the big blow-up that devastates a family. The first thing is to recognize that basic marital conflicts take place on different levels. Let's look at these levels and identify the level of *your* marital conflicts.

Blind fury

This is a marital conflict of the most destructive kind, a verbal "Gunsmoke shoot-out" where someone dies. Things are said not to inform but to hurt. Keep in mind that the thief, Satan, has come to steal, kill and destroy your marriage. Jesus has come that you might have life and have it more abundantly (See John 10:10).

A quarrel

A quarrel is not usually over the thing actually quarreled about. That's just the trigger. The gun was loaded over a period of time. If you listen during the quarrel, you will hear a lot that your partner feels is true about you though he hasn't said anything about it before to avoid hurting your feelings.

Brooding silence

This is conflict of the cold-war type. Nothing is being said; but watch out, it will be. Silence is a red light that says something is wrong. Hold a summit meeting. Discuss your differences. Avoid that hot war. Prayer makes a difference. Sometimes the biblical admonition is applicable here. If your enemy hungers, feed him, preferably his favorite dish or at her favorite restaurant. After settling back in an atmosphere conducive to sharing, talk about everything you can think of. Sooner or later the injury will come into the discussion. Let the other person bring it up. In the right conversational atmosphere, he will.

Disagreeable discussion about differences

A discussion becomes disagreeable when the topic under discussion becomes secondary as people attack each other. Instead of saying, "We can't afford that right now," the husband or wife will say, "How stupid can *you* get? Can't *you* add? We're out of money!" Agree in cooler moments to discuss *only* the subject. Anything else is fighting foul!

Agreeable discussion about differences

A pastor friend of mine tells each of the couples he marries to make a list of things they find objectionable about their marriage and exchange lists every Saturday morning over that second cup of coffee. That's a good idea!

What can you do about these conflicts? What can you do to reduce the level of tension?

Sometimes in our travels we come to a sign that says, "Dangerous, steep hill, shift to a lower gear." Learn to "gear down" your conflicts. Progress will come in stages, but at least it will come. If you can gear down blind fury to a quarrel, that's progress. If you can gear down a quarrel to golden silence, then considerate discussion, that's progress. If you can gear down silence to disagreeable discussion, at least you're talking, and that's progress. If you can gear down disagreeable discussion to agreeable discussion, that's the height of progress—and it's possible!

In his church study, a pastor once faced a husband who was filled with blind fury. His Christian wife had taken their children and left him. He was a backslider, had become abusive and had demanded that she engage in kinky sex practices. When she refused he told her she didn't love him. Things went from bad to worse until she left him and stayed with a church family.

The husband was a weight lifter, and while he was in the pastor's study, the two church secretaries had a prayer meeting in the hall for the pastor's safety!

The husband said to the pastor, "I demand to know where my wife is. If you don't tell me, I'll call the police."

The pastor replied, "There's the phone, help yourself. Talk to Police Chaplain Craft."

When the husband found out that he couldn't bully the pastor, who was more than two hundred pounds of muscle himself, he simmered down and began to talk. The pastor let him say whatever he wanted to and finally replied, "You know, your basic problem is spiritual. Your marriage will never make it without Jesus Christ."

After further counseling, the husband finally prayed. It was a mumbled prayer, but it was a start! The pastor sent for the man's wife, and the two were reunited in his office.

This pastor said, "Lowell, there is no couple in my church more in love or more faithful than this couple." The turning point came when the husband geared down from overbearing overdrive to the low gear of humility. Together, he and his wife were able to handle the mountains in their marriage.

Even better than gearing down conflicts is avoiding them altogether.

In our atomic power stations are complex alarm systems which go off when the reactors reach a danger limit. A normal rate of nuclear reaction produces power; a higher level threatens an explosion. Warning lights flash and an alarm sounds when there is an impending explosion.

Learn to tell from your mate's reaction whether your marriage combination is producing energy or threatening destruction. *Don't ignore the emotional warning lights!* Be honest, there may be a certain thrill in running red lights and playing chicken at an intersection, but too often a fatal collision is the result!

Many couples become locked into a collision course. Both regret the silly little thing that started it all, but neither wants to back down. Don't run red emotional lights unless you calculate the possible fatal consequences. What are the red lights? Here they are:

Replay of history

Some people collect hurts like others collect green stamps. When the book is full, it is cashed in and page after page is turned to show a full book.

Silence is golden here. When a pause does come, try to insert a humorous remark to show your mate that all attempts to bug you are unsuccessful.

Sarcastic humor

An example is a husband trying to intimidate his wife into losing weight. He says, "My wife should practice girth control." She retaliates, "My husband is flexible. He can put either foot in his mouth!" Everybody laughs except the person who recognizes a red light. Actually, the more he says the more resentful and insecure she feels; food is then her real friend and comfort.

Sarcastic humor is self-defeating.

Ignore it, or respond with real humor. Responding in kind will only add fuel to the fire. A soft answer turns away wrath (see Proverbs 15:1).

Grudging cooperation

One partner or the other says, "If I must do what you ask, I'm going to do it in a way that will take all the fun out of it for you!" This is a red light. To nag only entrenches the other person deeper in his resolve to drag his feet.

Foot-dragging is a way of retaliating. The worst thing you can do is make an issue out of it. Ignore the foot-dragging and try to do something nice to reward whatever cooperation you do get.

Brooding silence

Silence is not necessarily cooperation. It can be hostility camouflaged by phony and misleading compliance. Sooner or later the suppressed hostility will emerge as aggression, depression or departure.

Let's say you have seen the red light. You want to avoid a collision. You want to avoid an energy burn-out. During the Three-Mile Island atomic reactor crisis, the object was to "cool it"!

This is the quiet before the storm. *Remedy: Get your partner to talk about anything.* Conversation is the safety valve to take the pressure out of your mate's mood.

Someone has said that the fun goes out of a marriage when couples stop dating and start intimidating. The fun comes back in when couples stop intimidating and start initiating the kind of communication that gears down conflicts and then avoids them altogether.

CHAPTER FIVE

Heaven's View of You

God loves you just the way you are, but He loves you too much to *leave* you as you are! He has good things planned for you. God desires that you see yourself as an individual created in His image—as someone very special.

Marriage involves the person you see in your mind when you think of yourself. Let's call it your self-image. Whether or not you realize it, your self-image develops at a very early age. Psychologists say that a child is "signatured" by the age of 5.

Clare Booth Luce has this to say: "Many a girl in middle- and upper-class America is brought up to believe that she can remain a child (a sheltered dependent) her whole life long, on one condition: that she find a 'good man,' *i.e.*, a substitute for Daddy, to marry her. This husband-daddy, she is told, will give her a real doll's house to play house in, with real furniture in it and a real range to cook on; and, best of all, he will give her real, live dolls—babies—to play with. Early in life, she is taught to think of herself as a housewife and to expect that as a housewife she will 'belong' to her husband, just the way she belongs to Mommy and Daddy.

"As I have said, men, no less than women, subconsciously yearn to remain children all their lives. There is no way for a man to recapture childhood in the man's world—the world of work. So he, too, tends to seek it in marriage. To be sure, at the conscious level, a man is not only willing, he is eager to play the grown-up role of father-protector-provider to a child-wife and their children.

"But subconsciously he really wants to be the happy, selfish, waited-upon child himself, and he wants his wife to be his loving mommy. *A man's home may seem to be his castle on the outside; inside, it is more often his nursery.* And that's the main reason why most marriages are unhappy; each spouse wants to be the child and wants the other to be the parent.

"The honeymoon is always over when she says, 'Don't expect me to wait upon you like your mother,' and when he says, 'Look, you are not

Daddy's baby girl anymore. Act like a grown woman.' *Love in marriage seldom lasts unless both husband and wife are willing to behave like mature adults.*"

The immature adult may have suffered emotional setbacks during childhood. It is important that a child is loved and made to feel, "I'm somebody." If the child is abused, he feels, "I'm nobody." The nobody child grows into a nobody adult as far as self-esteem or self-image is concerned. The same principle works for the child who is loved, the somebody who grows up with a sense of self-worth.

So then a nobody adult falls in love with a somebody adult and they get married! The nobody adult feels inferior even though he may not be at all. In fact, he might be an individual of great accomplishment, having been driven by a sense of inferiority and determination to achieve great heights. Still, that nobody child is signatured inside this personality. Because his self-image has been formed that way, he has a terrible time overcoming it. This means that the key to happiness in your marriage may be in understanding your mate and helping him develop a sense of self-worth so he can, in turn, love you.

I know of one marriage where the husband came from a secure home and the wife was reared in a home where the father was an alcoholic. It took a lot of understanding for the husband to help his wife develop the self-confidence to become a creative, loving individual. He found that criticism was self-defeating. Love triumphed!

Let me illustrate the principle of how love shapes self-image. Scientists ran experiments with monkeys. They took baby monkeys and divided them into two groups. The monkeys in Group A were brought up in the normal "monkey way"—with mothers who loved, caressed and breast-fed them. The monkeys in Group B were presented with a stuffed mother monkey. They were fed with a balanced formula run through rubber nipples attached to the stuffed mother's breast.

The monkeys in Group A were fed and loved; the monkeys in Group B were fed but not loved. Both groups grew up, but the monkeys in Group A were somebodies, and having been loved, were lovers. The neglected monkeys in Group B grew up to hate their entire monkey world!

When the two groups were put together, the monkeys in Group A wanted sex and the monkeys in Group B didn't. When the female monkeys in Group B were finally subdued and later bore babies, they threw them against the bars of their cages!

What if someone could say to the nobody monkeys, "Look, physically and mentally you are as good as anyone"? Their reply would probably be, "But, we were unloved when we were growing up!" Now what if this person could say, "Yes, I know, but I love you. Let me love you—you're really lovable"? Do you know what would happen? The monkeys' self-esteem would change! Having changed, they would be capable of loving others.

This is why we need to get back to the basics. The Bible says *God loves you.* Keep saying, "God loves me," because He really does love you!

Frederick Drummer wrote a book entitled *Very Special People.* It is about people born with freakish infirmities. There was Francesco Lentini, who was born with three legs. Chang and Eng, twins, were joined at the chest for life. (They married sisters and fathered 22 children between them.)

There was the mule-faced woman who received several proposals for marriage, and the man she chose to be her husband was very handsome. All of these demonstrate the incredible ability of man's mind, soul and spirit to overcome physical imperfection. If you read Drummer's book you will never indulge in self-pity again. These people learned how to accept themselves.

How the monkeys thought about themselves determined their behavior. How the "very special people" thought about themselves determined their behavior. How you think of *yourself* determines *your* emotions and behavior!

In fact, *you feel what you believe.* If you want to change your feelings, *change what you think about yourself.* You are locked into a self-image by the self-created and self-perpetuated sentences you say to yourself.

Change your thinking and you will change the way you feel about yourself. "*As a man thinketh in his heart, so is he*" (Proverbs 23:7). Some people are victims of "stinkin' thinkin'." Others are happy because they accentuate the positive, eliminate the negative and don't mess with Mr. In-between.

Ray Stevens sings a song, "I'm Gonna Have a Little Talk with Myself." Have a little talk with yourself—but only after you've had a little talk with the Lord. Receive your self-image from Him. Allow God to love you as you are.

If you think your nose is too long or your shoe size too large, don't hate yourself. If you haven't achieved a doctorate in philosophy or aren't widely acclaimed as a virtuoso pianist, accept yourself. Once you have learned to respect yourself because you are God's child and His heir in Christ, you will have gained a special blessing. You will be able to follow His will and rejoice over what He accomplishes through you. You'll never be able to accomplish anything by declaring war on yourself—so learn to love and accept yourself. As Ray Stevens says,

Lately I have noticed all my friends avoiding me,
And the girl who loves me up and said good-bye.
My whole world is coming apart
    and falling in on me,
And I guess deep down I know the reason why.

Lately I've been living for nobody else but me;
Let my selfish ego take command.

Lately I've been giving in to pride and vanity,
And I guess I let it get the upper hand.

I think it's just about time to
    Have a little talk with myself,
    Have a little talk with myself—
A little private conversation,
A little self-examination,
A little attitude correction,
A little soul-searching inspection,
Start heading in the right direction,
Have a little walk, have a little talk with myself.

I put importance on the wrong things in this life,
And my outlook had a twisted point of view.
But all you reap with vanity
*   is heartache and strife,*
And without love and friendship
*   you can't make it through.* *

***Words and music by Ray Stevens. © 1969
Ahab Music Company, Inc.**

CHAPTER SIX

Heaven's Answer for Healing in Your Home

The Chinese have what they call the torture of a thousand cuts. Instead of killing the victim with one mighty thrust of a sword, they strap him down and, with a razor or knife, make 1,000 one- or two-inch cuts on his body. The victim doesn't die suddenly—he slowly seeps to death.

A lot of marriages die the same way—from a cutting remark here, a cutting statement there. Not one of the cuts is fatal in itself, but the cumulative effect of these little, cutting things is that love just seeps away.

When a marriage has been cut, healing must come from Heaven! God Himself has to touch hearts with forgiveness and restoration.

There has never been a perfect marriage, and the best marriages are welded together with love and forgiveness. Dr. R. Lofton Hudson has written a book about marriage entitled *Till Divorce Do Us Part*. In this helpful book he says, "True forgiveness is rare in this world, especially in the home. People forgive imperfectly, as we do everything else."

Dr. Hudson has counseled thousands of couples thinking of calling it quits. He made this observation: "When people ask me what the two biggest causes of divorce are, I feel like blurting out, anger and hate. There may be sexual infidelity, drunkenness, irresponsibility in money, mental cruelty, incompatibility—but these are often symptoms of deep-seated hostility. Labeling these responsive patterns does not change them.

"The basic problem in a large number of marriages which end in divorce is that one does not stop doing the offensive thing, and the other does not refrain from reacting, either outwardly or inwardly. In other words, divorce may come because two people spatter the mud of anger on each other so often, and it hardens into shells or crusts so thick, that these two people cannot get through to each other. They lose touch. They even quit feeling for each other."

Forgive your mate

Many marriages need forgiveness. Partners are so taken up with past hurts and resentments that any new problems that arise push them into a frenzy. If hurts are not forgiven quickly, they eventually lead to a breakdown of the marriage relationship.

It's hard to forgive! In fact, some find it almost impossible. This is where Christianity enables a husband and wife to find God's help. One out of two marriages ends in divorce, but a survey taken some years ago indicated that in cases where both husband and wife were active in church, read the Bible and prayed every day, the divorce rate was only one in 500.

The story is told of a husband who became involved with another woman and finally gathered the courage to confess his wrongdoing to his wife. He knew she would get angry and it would probably mean the end of the marriage, yet he felt he had to confess his guilt.

He said, "She sat, head in hands, until it was all out. Then she asked, 'Is it really true?' 'Yes,' I replied. 'And is that all?' I said, 'Yes.' The silence flowed by. Then she stood, stepped behind me and touched my hair. I looked up to see her eyes brimming with tears. 'I forgive you,' she said. 'Let's start over from here. Let's go on with life together.'"

Her response was too much for him to take. He trembled, and his teeth clicked before he could stop them, and his vision blurred.

"Why," she said in surprise, "you're angry." He nodded in admission. She said, "You wanted me to hit you, didn't you!"

Ruefully he admitted the truth. "No," his wife said, "I wouldn't hit you. That would only have justified everything you did. It might have touched off our tempers for the last time. No, I forgive you. Forgiveness is our only hope if we're ever going to live together again."

That was when the healing happened. Her forgiving him like that broke down his last resistance, his last feeling of self-justification. You see, he was still blaming her, her work and busy schedule for his unfaithfulness. Her forgiveness was so unexpected, it was as though she reached into resources he didn't know she had. She gave his life back to him.

Many sensitive people are deeply hurt by others who don't even realize the harm they have done. Jesus realized this, and when He was hanging on the cross and the soldiers were making a mockery of His death, He prayed, *"Father, forgive them, for they know not what they do"* (Luke 23:34). He forgave even though no one was asking for His precious forgiveness.

We should try to understand those who trespass against us because many people are still developing sensitivity to the feelings of others.

It is easy for your feelings to be hurt when you are young. I'll never forget the time when, as a boy, I was staying with my grandmother and several of her friends came to visit her. They were sitting in the living room having coffee when I happened to walk in. Grandma proudly introduced me. One of the ladies eyed me critically and said, "He sure is a skinny kid, isn't he?" Her words cut me like a knife. The worst part of it was that I knew she was right! She wasn't trying to hurt me. She was just speaking her mind.

Many insensitive people have never learned to pick their words like beautiful flowers. Some rough-talking husbands have turned their wives into bitter women. Callous, unthinking remarks hurt tender people. A country-western song describes a wife who says to her husband, "The only four-letter word you don't know is *love*."

Some days a person can take many things in stride which other days cut like a dagger. On Monday a man may joke with his wife about the dress she is wearing and she might laugh and reply, "Well, old baggy-pants, you don't look so sharp yourself." But if Tuesday is a terrible day and the children aren't feeling well, the washing machine has broken down and a cake has fallen flat, a critical remark by her husband might send her into tears.

We should forgive those who hurt us because they might not have intended their comments to hurt as deeply as they did. This is a difficult thing for parents to handle when they have several children. The temperament of each child is different, and it takes great wisdom to know how to handle each child. One child may take a spanking without a whimper; another will cry over a look of displeasure. We need to realize that adults react differently, too!

Leaders often have the diplomacy needed to correct people without hurting them, but this is not always true. Frequently a foreman will say something to an employee that hurts much more than was intended.

Forgive your superiors who hurt your feelings by what they say. If they knew how deeply they hurt you, they probably would word things differently. We are not free in every situation, but we are free to choose our attitude toward every situation.

How to forgive

Finally, you should forgive those who trespass against you. Even if they did intend to hurt you, you are going to injure yourself even more by thinking about the wrong they did to you. In other words, if someone stabs you with a comment, pull the dagger out and let the wound heal. Accept the release of forgiveness. It will enable you to live without resentment. If you harbor resentment, the hurt is amplified a thousand times. Some people have even suffered nervous breakdowns over wrongs they could not forgive.

Someone has said, "To return evil for good is like the devil does. To return evil for evil is like a man does. To return good for evil is like the Lord does."

It is often easier to talk about forgiveness than to forgive. Some people have been hurt so often that it would take a miracle of God for them to be able to forgive the people who have hurt them. A man who was a prisoner in China tells how his captors tormented him without mercy. His hatred grew until he realized how displeasing it was to the Lord. He began to pray for his tormentors and show them kindness whenever he could. Eventually they changed their attitude toward him and treated him kindly. His forgiveness of their evil actions worked for his own good.

During World War II, a serviceman was sent to the Philippines. His faithful wife stayed at home while her husband was stationed in this distant country. The man met a Filipino woman and fell in love with her. So he wrote a letter to his wife, asking her for a divorce.

She was crushed by the news, and bitterness filled her heart. Finally she granted him the divorce he wanted. Awhile later her ex-husband and his new wife had a baby daughter. Not long after that, he suddenly died of a heart attack. His Filipino wife and daughter were left without support and the wife found it nearly impossible to make a living. His first wife took compassion on them. She had found such release in forgiving her former husband that she asked the woman and her daughter to live with her. She supported them and helped the girl through college.

This woman was *free.* Forgiveness had released her from bitterness that might have poisoned her. She was released from the desire for revenge. She was released from self-pity and the nagging question, "Why did this have to happen to me?"

If your mate has hurt you and you have not forgiven him, allow yourself to experience the release of forgiveness. If God was willing to forgive you for your sins against Him, you should be willing to forgive your mate for his sins against you. Give up the poisonous memories filed in the back of your mind. Surrender to God and He will enable you to overcome feelings of bitterness.

This really works! Here is the testimony of a

woman who tried it:

"My husband was an alcoholic. I was a bitter Christian who was becoming an arthritic. I was a mother who resented what was happening to my girls. I saw doctors, a psychiatrist. No one could help me. Our home was about to break up. I was ready to get a divorce. Then a little old lady gave me the secret that transformed our home into heaven.

"I was telling her about my troubles and she said, 'Whenever you think of your husband, ask the Lord to *bless* him. The Bible says to love your enemies and bless those who curse you.'

"At first it was difficult. Bless the man who squandered our money on drink, then came home less than a husband and father? It was hard to do, but I did it. Gradually as I did, pity came into my heart, then compassion. Then I tried to do things to show God's love which I felt for him.

"To make a long story short, he became a Christian and quit drinking. And you know what? My arthritis disappeared! Ours became a happy home *when I did what the Bible said to do*."

We should forgive people *in our hearts* even if they do not ask for our forgiveness. When Jesus prayed, *"Father, forgive them,"* no one was asking for forgiveness! He was living and dying in the attitude of forgiveness.

When you forgive your mate, you will release your own feelings of bitter frustration. You can really accept yourself as a generous, forgiving person instead of someone just waiting to get even.

Be honest about your past

Forgive your past! Many people are in bondage to their past. If someone kicks a puppy often enough, that puppy will grow up with its tail between its legs and keep it there for the rest of its life, long after the kicking has stopped.

Some people were bruised in childhood. They are still in bondage to their traumatic experience. A wife was frigid and her husband wondered why. He learned that his wife's father had deliberately walked naked into his teen-aged daughter's bedroom. She was shocked, but even worse she carried this bad memory over into her married life.

There is only one release from a memory like that. That wife should forgive her father, see him forgiven in her heart, send that memory away, and love her husband.

There is release in forgiveness! Instead of holding grudges, release them through forgiveness. Why be a drudge to a grudge when you can forgive and really live!

CHAPTER SEVEN

Heaven's Way to Change Your Mate

After being married for three months, a husband went back to the minister who married him and said, "Reverend, I know I took her for better or worse—but it's worse than I thought!" I am sure many wives could say the same thing.

There are conflicts in marriage simply because people are different. Someone has said that marriage brings two people together, one who likes to sleep with the window open, the other who likes to sleep with it closed.

Do you remember the old rhyme, "Jack Sprat could eat no fat, his wife could eat no lean"? There are differences that mesh. Men and women are different. One person said, "Thank God for the difference!" How we handle our differences determines the degree of harmony in our homes. Some things can be changed—others cannot.

One husband I know has a six-hour sleep pattern; his wife has a nine-hour pattern. When they were first married, she would pull him back into bed to get him to match her pattern. But after he thrashed around restlessly for a few hours, she realized that she wasn't going to change him.

Studies have been made of sleep patterns which reveal they are as different as people are. Some people are larks and others are owls. Scientists found that it is dangerous to tamper with a person's sleep pattern. There are *some* things you cannot change.

My friend's wife finally realized this—and now he gets up early and rewards her consideration with a lingering embrace and coffee in bed at the time she needs to arise. A difference was turned into an advantage. She would have been foolish to insist on her way for his life. *Perhaps the best marriages are the ones in which people retain their individuality and learn to blend with each other's disposition.*

It is hard to resist the temptation to try and change your mate. Learn to differentiate between what you can and cannot change. Remember the prayer, "Dear God, grant me the serenity to accept the things I cannot change, courage to change the things I can and wisdom to know the difference." Once you know the difference, you can work on the things you *can* change.

The story is told of a bride who was waiting at the end of the aisle to make her entry. She saw the *aisle,* then the *altar,* then the *groom.* She thought as she looked at the scene, "I'll alter him," and after they were married she really tried.

How do you alter your mate?

Create a climate for change by changing yourself

Do something you don't like to do for him. Then ask him to do something for you. I once knew a couple who were very different. He loved automobile races; she hated them. She loved concerts; he was bored. Guess what? She went to the races then invited him to a concert. He went! Create a climate for change by changing yourself.

Create a climate for change, picking the opportune time to discuss changes

The wife who waits at the door with a list of chores to hand her husband as he enters is making a big mistake. Feed him first! Queen Esther banqueted King Ahasuerus before she made a request. She received what she asked for!

If your husband has romance in mind, if he has that look in his eye, don't turn him off with, "I hope you aren't getting any big ideas about tonight, hot shot," and then try to change something. It just won't work!

Create a climate for change in his life with compliments

If you want your mate to lose weight, have a big celebration if he loses two ounces! Really, criticism of an overweight person is translated, "I don't like you." The overweight person feels less secure and food becomes his friend. Criticism is self-defeating!

Create a climate for change through family and church worship

James says that wisdom that is from above is *"easy to be entreated"* (James 3:17). If two people have fellowship with God, they can have fellowship with each other. Trying to force a change in your mate when there is no fellowship with God is abortive. The Bible says, *"Love does not demand its own way"* (1 Corinthians 13:15).

If you want to change your mate, change yourself. A wife went to a lawyer and said, "I want to divorce my husband. In fact, I want to do more than that; I really want to hurt him."

The lawyer said, "Tell you what, if you really want to do that, set him up by being so kind, so loving and indulgent that when you file for divorce it will really get to him. Do that, and come back and see me in three months."

The months passed, and the client didn't appear. Finally the lawyer called her and said, "Why didn't you come in to follow through on your divorce?" She replied, "Divorce, nothing! I have one of the most wonderful marriages in the city." She changed the climate and changed her mate!

If a positive change is possible, so is a negative one. Husband, you might say, "I'm tired of trying. It's just not worth it." If you really felt that way you wouldn't be reading this book! Wife, you might be saying, "I'm tired of always giving in." Consider the alternative. To not try is to die. Refusing to try will strangle your marriage.

Thou shalt not kill

Today I killed my husband's love—
*   Not with a mighty blow;*
It had died bit by bit,
*   Year by year—so slow.*

First I robbed him of his pleasures
*   In those simple satisfactions.*

Oh, had he no self-confidence
  And some worthwhile ambitions?

I wounded him with cruel jibes
  When others, too, might hear
And thought his wince of pain
  Was but unmanly fear.

Tonight I saw the light of love
  Die slowly in his look,
When he reached toward me his hand,
  But I picked up my book.

Oh! God of the resurrection,
  Restore to me this man.
Then teach me how to truly love—
  And loving, understand.

You may not be able to control your mate, but you can control the climate. With a climate of forgiveness, love and praise, your mate will change.

Oh, incidentally, so will you!

CHAPTER EIGHT

Heaven's Way to Discipline Your Children

We are facing a phenomenon today. Parents are afraid of their children!

You don't believe it?

I just heard of a high school senior who threatened his mother, "Unless you buy me a car, I'm going to quit school." His mother gave in to the pressure and bought him a car. He wrecked the car and quit school anyway.

His younger brother, 16 years old, got the message and said to his mother, "Unless you buy me a car, I'm going to quit school."

By then she had had enough of this juvenile blackmail and replied, "Look, tomorrow you and I are going to take a trip to look over the boys' correctional institution. There are places for kids like you!"

That was the last she heard of the buy-me-a-car-or-else business. She learned a valuable lesson. *Concession to an unreasonable demand feeds aggression.*

Today, parents are afraid their kids won't love them, afraid their daughters will get pregnant. In fact, many mothers are providing their daughters with birth control information. Their logic is, "My daughter is going to have sex anyhow, and I don't want her to get pregnant, so I'll give her the pills!"

Parents are afraid their kids will get hooked on narcotics. One parental pastime is to go sniffing around the kids' rooms to check for marijuana.

These problems create pressure in a marriage. Even if nothing happens, the fear of trouble and tension over teen-agers returning home late take the fun out of a family.

One mother, hearing about the pregnancy of her only daughter, said, "I wish I were dead." Her husband told their pastor, "We just lie in bed at night and cry dry tears."

Is there any way to avoid this source of basic conflict? I think so. For many years, Dr. Spock advocated permissiveness and self-expression for children. Recently, however, he reversed his thinking and admitted he was wrong in omitting the kind of discipline the Bible talks about.

But it was too late to help in many homes where unmanageable situations had already developed.

Second to the lack of discipline in families is the lack of time parents spend with their kids. Let's look at these two basic causes of conflict.

When Carl Malz joined the Lundstrom Ministries, he moved up from Texas with a cat, three dogs, a horse and a colt. He and his wife, Betty, bought a small farm west of Sisseton.

The horses got away and ran down the road. The colt got tangled and cut in some old barbed wire. One of the pedigreed collies ran out onto the road and was hit by a car. Now the collie's two hind legs are paralyzed, at least temporarily.

"Good grief!" Carl says, "One thing I've learned in a situation like this is to put up my fences first! I mean right away!" The fences were finally put up, but not before damage was done to the animals.

God has given us fences. The Ten Commandments are part of His fencing. Another part of His fencing consists of parental responsibility in setting limits on what children can and cannot do. Psychologists tell us that children expect this and will push us until we erect a fence.

A good way to spoil a child is to do everything to avoid a conflict. That kind of child says,

"Mother did everything for me from the time I was little. Why should I stop expecting it now?"

Knowledgeable parents start setting limits (fences) on the behavior of their children early in life. In setting reasonable limits, it is best to be direct and absolute concerning what can and cannot be tolerated.

If parents are afraid to risk a child's displeasure by setting limits, the child will go overboard until his parents get the "I-want-limits" message. If the parents fail to get the message, the child will face painful lessons in an unloving and far-from-permissive world.

The dean of Trinity Bible Institute in Ellendale, North Dakota, once said, "Kids who come to us from homes without discipline say to me, 'Why didn't my parents ever make me obey? Now I'm in a school with rules, and it's really hard on me!'"

The fact is, it takes more love, time and heartache to *train* a child in the way he *should* go than to let him do his own thing. It takes more time to cultivate a garden than to raise weeds!

When you determine to reinstate authority in your home, be sure to temper it with a lot of time and attention. It will be worth it. Conflicts may be unavoidable, but conflicts over standards are better than the false peace that only delays the moment of a greater confrontation.

You must build fences for your family if tragedy is to be averted. Love without parental authority transfers authority to the child. The commandment gets changed to "Parents, obey your children if you love them!" It doesn't work.

I know many Christian parents who allow their children to have their own way. The tranquility of their homes is shattered by loud rock 'n' roll music. The TV blares until all hours of the night. Church attendance is not mandatory, so their teen-agers do not attend the house of God.

In one of the families operated in this way, three of four kids became hooked on drugs. One met a tragic death. Another went to prison and was saved there. Thank God for the salvation experience! These parents loved their children, but not enough to discipline them. Now it's almost too late.

Love and authority fit into God's biblical pattern for the home—*but Mom and Dad must stand together on discipline.* A study in New York City revealed that the perfect incubator for rearing a delinquent was a home in which one parent was strict and the other indulgent.

The kids interpreted their parents' behavior like this, "Mr. Mean is mistreating me because he won't let me do what I want to, yet Mom says it's okay. I hate authority!"

The approach must be, "Because I love you,

you must obey me." You need to clearly define what you expect from your youngster and stick to it—no wobbly fences. Then, when you spend time with your child, you build a bridge of love over which your child will walk in obedience. Finally, expect your lines of authority—your fences—to be tested! Your child will test you just as you tested your parents! Don't give in if demands are unreasonable.

Dr. Spock says, "Parental submissiveness only encourages children to be more pesky and demanding, which in turn makes the parent increasingly resentful until this finally explodes in a display of anger, great or small, that convinces a child to give in. In other words, *parental submissiveness doesn't avoid unpleasantness; it makes it inevitable.*"

This explosive display of anger leaves its own residue of resentment. Discipline your child when you have yourself under control, and love the youngster afterward. He will feel secure inside the fence, and you will be glad you loved him enough to build the fence. Avoid the "Other kids do it—why can't I?" influence. Build your fence with the Word of God!

I believe in discipline. I have found that parents who are firm in the application of discipline need to discipline far less than parents who make and change rules every day. Children who know how far they can go will stop short of decisive action from a parent. I would always warn our children after the first offense. The second offense brought five swats with the belt on the buttocks, the third offense ten, the fourth 15, and so on. The children seldom chose to disobey more than 15 swats' worth! I often read the Scripture first, showing them that God expected me to protect them against their stubborn, willful ways. Then, after reading the Scripture, they would get their five swats, and then we would have prayer. Connie and I would always take them in our arms afterward and hug them until they had quieted down emotionally.

An excellent book on this subject is *Dare to Discipline*, by Dr. James Dobson. It has sold more than one million copies. Another book, *The Strong-Willed Child*, by the same author, is a must for every parent facing the challenges of child rearing.

It's difficult to believe, but some Christian parents play games with each other. They use their children to get their own way, not realizing they are breeding rebellion in the children.

Mom and Dad, get together on this matter of love and authority by coming under God's authority yourselves. Then spend time with your children. It's the only way to build the bridge of love over which all of you must walk.

Brooks Adams was the son of Charles Francis Adams, Lincoln's ambassador to Ireland. His dad *took time* from his busy schedule to go fishing with his son. The 8-year-old Brooks wrote, "Went fishing with my dad—greatest day in my life." He made reference to that great day for 40 years. Charles Francis Adams, the father, wrote in his diary under the same date, "Went fishing with my son—a day wasted." *Was it?* Children are a treasure of the Lord. Just as people often waste their money, they often waste their children. Few people really realize the principles needed in rearing chilren.

Make certain that your own commitment to Christ is complete

Children need a godly example because they are born imitators. A child is an everlasting soul, and his greatest need is to see God in his mom and dad. When children see Mom and Dad loving God only partially and putting the Kingdom of God second, they assume the Lord isn't important enough to come *first*. This will open up the children to all kinds of compromises. Because they have not learned how to resist temptation, they may fall into the pit of destruction.

Mom and Dad, if you want your children to be saved, get away from sin as fast as you can. Serve the Lord with all your heart; this will make a lasting impression upon your children!

Make certain your children know the Word of God

A child needs to learn spiritual habits. I have noticed that some of the sternest disciplinarians often rear children who depart from the Christian faith as soon as they enter college or get away from home. It dawned on me a few years ago that many children have never formed their own spiritual habits. They have conformed to the family devotions, to the spiritual regulations set forth by their parents, but they haven't formed a way of life on their own.

The Psalmist David said, *"Thy Word have I hid in my heart that I might not sin against thee"* (Psalm 119:11). God's Word is a deterrent to immorality, and it is the father's responsibility to be sure the children are taught the Bible. Dad, you had better be a man of God's Word. Teach your children the Bible, and you will see them grow into strong Christians.

Prepare your children for the moral decisions they will have to make

Many Christian families have a continual discussion going on about the moral events and questions of the day. Does your family discuss the pros and cons of smoking, drinking, drugs, war, abortion, pre-marital sex, divorce, racial discrimination, and other controversies and questions of our day?

So much table talk in Christian homes borders on gossip. Don't argue over the petty problems of the household. Prepare your sons and daughters for the temptations they must face in the future. For example, there is an article in the March, 1979, *Good Housekeeping* magazine, "How I Got My Daughter to Stop Smoking Pot." Get it from the library—it's great! Read it, discuss it, immunize your children!

Give your children a sense of honor and destiny

Dr. Robert Schuller is minister of the Garden Grove Community Church in California and is the featured speaker on the popular "Hour of Power" television program. He and Arvella, his wife, have five children who love the Lord. Dr. Schuller's philosophy of family relationships is this: the family is a mini-nation, a tiny town, a tiny state, with legislative, judicial, and executive branches and duties. The husband is the king, the wife the queen, sons are princes, and daughters are princesses.

The children are taught to be ambassadors-at-large for the Schuller family, wherever they might be. From childhood, they are encouraged to be at their best when they are away from home or on their own. Dr. Schuller says, "We've always tried to build a sense of self-esteem and dignity with our children."

This is the secret of a successful family—self-esteem and dignity. If you tell your child he is stupid, he will grow up convinced that he is stupid. If you speak to a child as though he is a rebel, unworthy of respect and untrustworthy, chances are he will conform to your impression of him.

A child needs an apology

Learning to say "I'm sorry," is one of the most difficult things a parent can do, but it is also effective. When I've misjudged the children or said something to my wife that I shouldn't have, I've always tried to apologize. Because I try to be honest, my children know they rest securely in my love, and they love me in turn.

If you are not serving God as you should, whatever you sow you are going to reap. It will be a bitter harvest if your child makes hell for himself in this world and in the world to come. As a parent, the best decision you could ever make is to give your heart to God fully so your child will learn how to pray and to love God forever.

CHAPTER NINE

Heaven's Laws
for In-Laws

By Betty Malz

I've been blessed with wonderful in-laws and have experienced few of the problems that are the cause of so many troubled marriages. But in counseling with hundreds of couples who have attended our Family Life Seminars, I have found that interference by parents and other relatives is a common source of friction and unhappiness. Often two people who are ideally suited to each other find it difficult, if not impossible, to build a life together that pleases them and their in-laws at the same time.

Betty Malz, wife of associate evangelist Carl Malz, wrote about some of the mother-in-law problems of her first marriage in her best-selling book, My Glimpse of Eternity. *With God's help, those problems were solved. In fact, even after the death of her first husband, his mother has remained a very dear and special friend.*

Because of this experience and her own deep insight and wisdom, I've asked Betty to write this chapter.

—Lowell Lundstrom

I understand that the Bible teaches that $1+1=1$. *"The two shall become as one"* (See Mark 10:7). But when two people marry, they inherit four in-laws. That makes a combination of six people working to make that family union a happy (?) one.

The Scripture says that when a man marries he shall forsake his father and mother and cling only to his wife. The trouble comes either early or late, when the new husband or wife tries to bring about this change too suddenly by isolating his or her partner totally from the family.

In most cases, the wife has the most difficult time breaking the ties with her family. Husband, don't judge her too harshly—she did give up her last name to assume yours. Help her, encourage her and love her into behaving nicely, for whatever she does from now on, she does in *your* name. If she dies trying to make your marriage work, let's face it—your last name will be on her tombstone!

I was terribly jealous of my mother-in-law. She could outcook me and was as smart as a tree full of owls. But, then, she had a 40-year start on me. Mothers-in-law are sometimes like employers who won't hire young people without experience. You don't attain experience unless someone gives you the chance to get it.

One day I realized that the woman I resented and her husband, my father-in-law, were not all that bad or they could never have produced the charming young man I fell in love with. I believed this to such an extent that I left the parents I loved, who had invested 19 years of love and expense in me, to promise to live with him for the rest of my life. *If it were not for your in-laws, you would not have your mate at all. You owe them respect and appreciation.*

Most people don't fully realize this until they have a baby girl or boy who grows up to leave the nest. They are worried that their precious child may find a mate who will not cherish him and perhaps be unkind or cruelly unfair.

My grandfather used to say, "Blood is thicker than water." Even though my new husband almost worshiped me, the blood that flowed through his veins was the same blood that flowed through the veins of my in-laws. In a sense, he owed them his life. I came to realize that the kind of love a boy has for his mother is not the same variety of love he has for his wife.

I also learned that if I really wanted my husband's total love, I must love his mother. It was not easy—she was not naturally lovable. Her religion, background, customs and outlook were all different from mine. That was not her fault. I forgot that, from her perspective, my ways were just as different.

I had two choices: to change my mind or change the location of our home. In rare cases this is necessary. Two years after my husband and I were married, we did invest in a business 124 miles away. After moving away, it was refreshing to be treated as a loving guest in my mother-in-law's home instead of a competitor for the love of her son.

But before that happened, there were many adjustments to be made. My husband shocked me one morning over coffee. We were sitting close together in our breakfast booth, cherishing the last five minutes before he left for work. He kissed me on the cheek and said, "Beginning Monday morning we will apply the Golden Rule here at our house. I will treat your mother exactly the way you treat mine. I will go to see your mother as often as you visit mine."

He was so easy-going, never complaining, I didn't think he had noticed that I made sure the baby saw my mother more than his. I had wanted her to become more attached to my people than his.

When he left, I cried. I only cry about once every two years, whether I need to or not, but I cried that morning. My husband had torn up my playhouse. He had seen the game I was playing but loved me too much to criticize me for doing it. I stopped crying, mused, began thinking realistically, and prayed.

I recalled how cute my mother thought it was that I had my husband so henpecked that he would jump and bow to my commands. Yet she thought it a tragedy when my brother got married and his wife treated her son the same way I treated her son-in-law. *"Do unto others as you would have them do unto you"* (See Luke 6:31). It hit me—the Ten Commandments would not have been needed if the world obeyed the Golden Rule.

It was up to me. Our marriage would be a *duel* or a *duet*. The choice usually rests with the in-law (bride or groom) coming into the family of the spouse.

I was not the only person at fault. My mother-in-law insisted that my husband stop by her house on the way home from work each evening instead of coming home to me first. So I decided to call her and tell her off. Since she was a religious woman, I sat by the phone and picked up my Bible, looking for some verse I could use on her. I decided that I would find the Scripture verse, *"Jealousy is as cruel as the grave"* (Song of Solomon 8:6). That would put her in her place! Then it dawned on me—the reason I could recognize jealousy so readily was that I was experienced in the subject. I had majored in jealousy and minored in understanding.

Determined to impress her with the Word, my sword, I searched for that verse, but instead found another: *"Set a watch, O Lord, before my mouth; keep the door of my lips"* (Psalm 141:3). Feeling very ashamed, I put the receiver back on the hook and never made that hurtful, accusing phone call.

I began to realize that I could either *unite* or *untie* my marriage by my attitude. The words "unite" and "untie" are spelled with the same letters, the only difference being the position of the "I" (little i, in my case). The word unite means "to combine or put together"; the word untie means "to separate."

In-law trouble can fray the rope that ties a couple together, and a frayed rope carries little weight. Keep the ties strong that bind you and your mate together. Refuse to allow anything or anybody to wear away at them until they are weak and easily broken. Remember that people do not make you happy or unhappy. Happy is something you *are*. In-laws cannot make you un-happy unless you allow them to. People can only hurt you if you permit their offense to touch you.

Don't point out your in-laws' faults to your mate. He lived with them 20 years and knows them better than you do. You're not hurting the in-laws; they couldn't care less for your opinion. All you do is turn your mate against you; so pray for them instead. God can do more in ten min-utes than you can accomplish in ten years of talking.

Misunderstanding, resentment, hate and jeal-ousy can rob you of energy and actually make you ill. When two strong people push against each other over an issue as volatile as in-laws, both are paralyzed. But, even two weak individ-uals pulling together, pushing in the same direc-tion, become an energizing force. As the Scripture says, *"One shall chase a thousand, and two put ten thousand to flight"* (See Deuter-onomy 32:30). Nothing can stop a couple's love or their efforts when they are *"laborers together with God"* (1 Corinthians 3:9).

In some extreme cases, couples have to move away from parents to become grown-up indi-viduals. This need not be an alienation from parents. Frequent letters, short phone calls, notes, and occasional short visits are far better than an antagonistic relationship with them.

Remember, too, that there are two sides to every story. In-laws are not always the people at fault in a situation. My mother-in-law worked hard to prepare a great Sunday meal to keep me from getting up earlier on Sunday morning. She saved me a great deal of time and money, yet I resented it when she asked the price of things I bought. When the prying got too bad, I learned to answer her question, "How much did you pay for those drapes?" with, "Not as much as you would think," or, "About half what they usually cost." She got the message without my telling her it was none of her business.

Some couples beg their in-laws for money, or loans, then stick their tongues out at them when they ask for a little attention, time, or physical help with some chore around the property. Keep in mind, nothing in life is *free!* If a couple accepts free babysitting and free meals, they must be prepared to accept free advice.

If you must borrow money from in-laws, offer to pay it back, and *do* so even if it is at the rate of $2 per week. If you never get it paid off, at least your payments cancel the idea that you are not trying.

Helping people is not always easy. I never fully sympathized with in-laws until I found myself in that role. I discovered that sometimes in-laws should send money to their children anonymously to keep wrong or awkward relationships from developing. I remember when my daughter needed her teeth fixed. My son-in-law was still in college and did not have the funds to take care of this need. Our offering to pay for her dental expenses would have insulted him. Our daughter would not have accepted the money because she wanted us to respect her husband, who was doing the best he possibly could to take care of her.

So my husband and I went to the dentist and worked out an arrangement with him. He contacted our daughter and told her that an anonymous donor had offered to take care of her dental care without charge to her or her husband. He explained that the donor was interested in furthering the education of promising students. Making such an arrangement helps clarify your own motives in your mind. Do you really want to *help* or *buy* your children by obligating them?

Be sure your motives are pure when you give to your struggling children. Sometimes there is strength in struggle. If a baby chick is helped out of the shell, its muscles will never develop. A child's skull bones close in properly as a result of the pressure against the pelvis of the mother as the baby struggles to emerge from the womb into the "real world."

There are exceptions. If parents see that their

children have had a reversal or crisis, they may have to help to keep them from going without needed medication, proper food, or to keep them from losing their home. Parents need to beware, however, for some young people deliberately get themselves into a "bind" to get the sympathetic "bail." Parents must be realistic and pray for God's wisdom and guidance in these matters to avoid being manipulated.

Last, but not least, preserve the happiness of your home once your children are married. You can't live your children's lives for them—don't jeopardize your own marriage trying.

CHAPTER TEN

Heaven's Way
to Stretch Your Pay

I suppose everybody has heard the old challenge—"Put your money where your mouth is." The truth is that, in most cases, your mouth is where your money is! Out of the abundance of the heart the mouth speaks and the hand reaches.

What do you talk about when you talk about money? Investing in God's Kingdom? Keeping up with your friends? Investigating how to spend it wisely? These are revealing questions because the answers we give identify us. I believe it is impossible to separate money from what we are or where we are with God.

We cannot separate money from what we are. Oftentimes, people are poor because they have poor ways.

Poverty-minded people never learn how to

spend money. A friend who is the manager of a grocery store tells me that many people who come in with government food stamps buy junk food like pop and potato chips instead of the more nourishing kinds of food. They have poor ways.

Here are some types of people who express themselves in different ways with their money.

The *big spender* is happy, jolly and fun-filled. Girls love this kind of boyfriend. But after marriage, he turns out to be a better playmate than a thrifty mate.

The *depressed shopper* goes shopping to cheer herself up. She cures the blues, but puts her husband in the red.

The *gambler* takes his chances with money, love and life. He always has a big deal coming— a long way off—so why worry about today? Team this man with a frugal wife and you have chaos! He loans money on long shots and ends up with bucks shot and short bucks.

The *impulse buyer* is completely unpredictable. He may save pop bottles for the deposits, plan strange menus to use up off-brand coupons, and be so penny-pinching that everybody's life is made miserable. Then, on an impulse, this person spends a scandalous amount of money without doing any investigative homework! This person will be impulsive in other ways, too, because you cannot separate money from what you are.

Oh yes, and then there's the *tightwad*. He's a carefree type. He doesn't care—as long as it's free! When he goes out with his friends for dinner, he leaves the table first, before the check arrives. He is known as an "after dinner sneaker." When December comes, he "dreams of a tight Christmas." He's a man of rare gifts. When he gives, it's rare!

We cannot separate money from who we are or where we are with God. So when we talk about money problems, we are really talking about a person's relationship to the Lord.

An unnamed author wrote, "I dreamed that the Lord took my Sunday offering and multiplied it by ten. This amount became my weekly income. In almost no time I lost my color TV, had to give up my new car and couldn't even make my house payments. What can a fellow do with $50 a week?"

If the Lord multiplied your weekly offering by ten and made that your weekly income, how much would you make? I have news for you: God has a key of prosperity for you and your family!

"When the Lord guides, He provides
And when He leads, He feeds."

To solve your money problems, start with God's success formula, *"This book of the law shall not depart out of thy mouth, but thou shalt meditate therein day and night, that thou mayest observe to do according to all that is written therein; for then thou shalt make thy way prosperous, and then thou shalt have good success"* (Joshua 1:8).

God has a formula for success. He told Joshua, *"You shall make your way prosperous."* Sometimes Christians ask God to prosper them and then leave it all up to Him. Joshua had to struggle with his enemies, but God was with him. You may have to struggle at times, but God will prosper you, too.

The four natural laws of prosperity

There are four natural laws of prosperity, and they will work for anyone. This is why the sinner who uses these laws is more prosperous than the Christian who doesn't.

Let me ask you some questions:

How do you manage your time? Managing your time is managing your life. Hours can be wasted in front of a TV set. In fact, it has been estimated that the average person spends nine years out of his life watching TV!

How do you manage your mind? The mind makes the body rich. Leaders are readers. Have you ever heard of Eric Hoffer? For years he was a drunken bum. At times he would help unload ships in San Francisco to earn some money. He started reading. He read his way all the way to a professorship at the University of Southern California! He discovered a natural law of prosperity. If you want to lead—read!

How do you manage your relationships? Do you hang around people who sing a "someone-did-me-wrong" song? Losers hang around with losers. Choose your friends carefully. Choose friends who are problem-solvers. I want to be with people who talk about the Lord, men and women of faith who believe in exciting possibilities. Have you ever listened to the average conversation? Good grief! Where are the mind-expanding thoughts that inspire? When you find someone who challenges your faith and mind, hang on to that friend. He will help you improve yourself.

How do you manage your money? Are you an impulse buyer? Home economists advise you to never go grocery shopping when you're hungry; too many things will look good. When you shop, go alone. Have you ever seen kids—or husbands—piling unnecessary items into the grocery cart at a supermarket?

Do you shop for low interest rates when you get a loan? Bank-interest notes are usually lower than a car dealer's. A bank loan is usually cheaper than a loan-company loan. Don't be afraid of the banker—your interest pays his wages! He really wants to be your friend.

Do you shop for insurance? Talk to someone who knows how to handle money or buy *Sylvia Porter's Moneybook* in paperback. It will save you thousands of dollars.

These are the natural laws of prosperity. People use them every day on the road to financial freedom.

For the Christian, there is a big advantage. In addition to the four natural laws which people work for themselves, there are four spiritual laws which put God's blessing on his side.

The first law of spiritual prosperity is that God owns everything

A Christian doesn't own anything. We only manage money for God.

Second, God is your source of supernatural wealth

The Bible teaches us that God owns the cattle on a thousand hills. The earth is the Lord's and the fullness thereof (See Psalm 50:10 and Deuteronomy 10:14). By the act of His will, God can bless you with more in a moment than you could earn in a lifetime.

Dr. Robert Schuller says, "People don't have money problems. They have *thought* problems." God can give you a divine thought, an idea, a plan, a promotion, a gift, that can prosper you more than all your fleshly efforts.

Third, God rewards your giving

Jesus said, *"Give, and it shall be given unto you; good measure, pressed down, and shaken together, and running over, shall men give into your bosom. For with the same measure that ye mete withal it shall be measured to you again"* (Luke 6:38). As you give to God, *"shall men give into your bosom."* He will cause your path to cross with the right person at the right time, so it will happen.

Fourth, invest by faith

Plant some "seed" by faith giving. The Bible says we should give freely and what we give will determine what we get out of life! *"He which soweth sparingly shall reap also sparingly; and he which soweth bountifully shall reap also bountifully"* (2 Corinthians 9:6). You can actually *give* your way to prosperity. Give to your church, give to missions, give to soul-winning efforts like the Lundstrom ministry—and see what happens! Investing by faith will bring an inflow of financial blessing to your life.

Now let's talk about how you handle money. The Bible says if you're going to build a tower (or a home), count the cost. Figure it out. You can't spend what you don't have. The mismanagement of money is one of the largest causes of divorce in America today.

Let me give you a few suggestions about family finances. In almost every marriage, one member is usually better at handling funds than the other. I know of one family where the husband complained about the way his wife was handling the funds, so she gave him the checkbook. After a month he was happy to turn all that bill-paying back to her!

On the other hand, there are some wives who can't handle money, or even balance a checkbook. *Decide who should be the family treasurer.* Then decide how the money will be spent. I know of one family where the working wife pays the household bills from her account and the husband claims that all the money in his account belongs just to him!

Second, *figure your income for the year on the basis of one primary income.* Many marriages go down the tube because long-term debts are built up based on two incomes. If something happens to one partner's earnings, the loss of income sinks the ship.

Third, *divide large annual expenditures (insurance, income tax, etc.) by 12 and set that amount of money aside each month in a separate fund so that you do not have to go and get a loan when these expenses come due.*

Budget your other gifts and expenses. Count the cost. For instance, you might be amazed at what you spend each month to eat at restaurants. If you eat out frequently, can you really afford it?

Next, *throw away your credit cards.* It will be tough for awhile, but you will feel better when the big bills *don't arrive!* I call this plastic surgery.

Avoid competing with your neighbors (or relatives) for material accumulations, such as the most expensive car on the block and the biggest and best refrigerator-freezer. The harmony of your home is of more value than anything else. Debt is a yoke. Unreasonable debt can depress a marriage. If you're in a debt mess, write or talk to each creditor and tell him you will pay him a little each month. Then he will at least know you intend to pay him.

Husband, avoid any expenditure that will take food off of the table or an occasional new dress off the back of your wife. Wife, avoid diverting family funds to continually bail out that son or daughter who hasn't learned to handle money or do without. You're merely feeding personal self-indulgence. It may be hard, but some kids have to bottom-out on their finances before they grow up.

Learn to live on less than you make. It is vitally important to save regularly for your "rainy day." Pay yourself first in a savings account.

Finally, *learn the great lesson that having "more" is not a guarantee of happiness.* The Bible says, *"He that loveth silver shall not be satisfied with silver, nor he that loveth abundance, with increase"* (Ecclesiastes 5:10). We are living in the days of discontent. Learn to love people and use things, not love things and use people.

Sylvia Porter says, "We are into an 'era of aspirations' in our economy. In this era, most of us will spend a shrinking share of our income on the traditional necessities of food, clothing, shelter, and transportation while we spend a steadily increasing share of our income for goods and services which reflect our hopes and wants."

Dr. George Katona says, "If what you have today appears insufficient tomorrow, disappointment and frustration may become frequent occurrences. Stress, tension and anxiety may even grow far beyond what has prevailed in less affluent societies. *The higher the aspirations, the more chance that people will be disappointed."*

You might have to follow the example of the fellow who said, "Give me the small size. I can't afford the large, economy size!"

Money problems are a lot like diet problems. We know what we should do, but it's really tough to cut back in a day of credit smorgasbords. (Let's call them *more-gasbords.*) Someone has said that inside of every fat person is a thin person trying to get out. He eats because of inner frustration. The same is true of the spender. He spends to satisfy his frustrations. Beware of your emotions. They could drive you to the poor house!

CHAPTER ELEVEN

Heaven's Plan
for the Married Man

Some friends of ours lived next to a henpecked husband. Month after month they listened to his wife's verbal tirades. One day this couple was in the back yard, and she was at it again. Her husband finally spoke up and said, "Myrtle, I don't mind your telling me what to do, but please don't put your hands on your hips!"

What has happened to the male image in a society affected by Women's Lib? We are part of a culture that depreciates men, from the bungling husband in cartoons to the naive ignoramus in TV ads, which are slanted toward women because they do most of the buying. After all this belittlement, it is no wonder that a TV comedian has arrived at stardom by getting laughs with his joke line, "I don't get no respect." Dr. E. E. LeMasters, in a report published by

UNESCO, writes sadly, "The man is no longer king of his castle: there has been a court revolution, and the father has emerged as the court jester."

Husband, take a second look at your mother. Chances are she was the dominant person in the family in which you grew up. You were probably programmed to have a dominant female around; and when you met one, you fell for her because you felt at home with someone like your mother. This isn't my analysis; this represents the considered opinion of experts on this subject.

Even so, it's better to fight for what's right than to switch. I know of a fellow who used to turn his entire paycheck over to his wife and then have to ask her for money. He finally wised up, cashed his own check and took out what he really needed. Then he turned the rest over to his wife, who was a wise and thrifty bookkeeper. She respected him for it.

Sir, your wife would be happy for you to assert your manhood in the right place. If you are like some men, you're depressed because of suppressed resentment. Learn to laugh at your situation. Tell the whole family, "Never fear, underdog is here!" Then turn into a superdog and come up with a performance they will admire.

Earn the respect of your wife. No woman can really respect a husband who leaves to her the responsibilities of rearing the family, attending church and disciplining the children.

The Bible teaches that the man is the head of the house and the priest of the family. He is the spiritual leader who determines the image of God which comes into the minds of children when they call Him "Heavenly Father." Sir, you would be amazed at the change in your household if you would assume your God-designated responsibilities and start to lead. A wife wants a head, not a tail, in spiritual matters. Take time to provide spiritual guidance for your family.

As a counselor as well as an evangelist, I have talked to hundreds of families that were about to break up. In most cases, when the husband established the right relationship with God, things began to fall into place. In fact, it became apparent afterward that part of the henpecking resulted from the husband's evasion of his role. His wife was poking at him in the same way you poke at a fireplace log, hoping to get a little fire. When the fire is burning, there's no need to poke!

In Shakespeare's play, "The Taming of the Shrew," Petruchio, who is looking for a wife, is told by Hortensio about a lass who is rich, young and beautiful. She is Katherine Minola, who is "renowned in Padero for her scolding tongue."

Upon meeting her, he could have said, like

some men, "I was told she was all peaches and cream, but I found out she was all screeches and scream." How does Petruchio avert becoming a henpecked husband? He compliments her lavishly. He matches her contention with his own until friends say, "Did you ever see the like. He kills her in her own humour." To say it in another way, he outplays her at her own game. But senseless ranting dosn't prevail—the contention is humorous, but fair. Petruchio summarizes his method:

"This is a way to kill a wife with kindness
And thus I'll curb her mad and headstrong
  humour,
He that knows better how to tame a shrew
Now let him speak; 'tis charity to show."

Katherine, later tamed, has a word for women:

"Even such a woman oweth to her husband;
And when she's forward, peevish, sullen, sour
And not obedient to his honest will,
What is she but a foul, contending rebel
And graceless traitor to her loving lord."

Not all men have the skill or are as successful as Petruchio! Abraham Lincoln is revered as a gentle man and yet a president of towering greatness. He was married to a woman who had a keen mind, a selfish disposition, great ambition, and little love. One historian comments that Lincoln's unhappy marriage to Mary Todd lasted 22 years, and during the last of those years Lincoln's wife ran up embarrassing bills, flew into jealous rages and made no secret of their differences.

A Springfield neighbor told of having seen Mrs. Lincoln, with a knife in her hand, chasing her husband down the street. He suddenly turned on her and hustled her into the house, spanking her and saying, "There, now come in the house, and don't disgrace us before the eyes of the world."

He did not let his home life cripple his success in politics. In fact, there are some who believe that his domestic life drove him out of the house, into politics and into the presidency. Mrs. Lincoln, as the wife of the president, still tried to run the show. With his disarming sense of humor, Lincoln called her "Mrs. President."

Her poor disposition only heightened his greatness. At a dinner party given by the president for General Grant and his officers, Mrs. Lincoln first attacked General Grant and then her husband in a tirade horrifying the officers. As described by an official attendant:

"The president bore it as Christ might have done, with an expression of pain and sadness

that cut one to the heart, but with supreme calmness and dignity. He called her 'Mother' with his old-time plainness; he pleaded with eyes and tones, and endeavored to explain or palliate the offenses of others until she turned on him like a tigress; and then he walked away, hiding that noble, ugly face that we might not catch the full impression of its misery."

Petruchio tamed his shrew, and Lincoln rose above his in towering greatness. Neither bowed!

CHAPTER TWELVE

Heaven's Wisdom for Married Women

Webster's Dictionary says that a martyr is one who sacrifices his life for the sake of a principle. In 1 Samuel 25, we read the story of Abigail, a brainy, beautiful wife married to a bickering, bullheaded boozer. She had the chance of a lifetime to get rid of him because David wanted to kill him. Instead, she pled for the life of her husband, Nabal. Later, Nabal died. David, who had been impressed by this woman of principle, sent for her and took her to be his wife.

We live in a throw-away society. One of the latest innovations is a paper, throw-away wedding dress. It is almost representative of how seriously some people take the vow, "for better or worse."

A survey was taken recently of people who had been divorced. They were asked, "Did you really try to make your marriage work out?" About seventy percent said they had not put much effort into making their marriages work. It was easier to run from the problems than face them!

But there are many women who, like Abigail, refuse a shortcut out of their unhappy marriages. They are women of principle and conviction, who trust God. They not only keep on, but do so in such a way that others admire them for it.

Nabal was a wealthy man but a poor husband. Sometimes a wife conceals her heartbreak under an outward show of respectability. Laying the political issues aside, for I cannot agree with some of her decisions, one of the great women of a recent era was Eleanor Roosevelt, wife of the late president, Franklin Delano Roosevelt. Her disadvantages were monumental. Born to a beautiful mother, people said of Eleanor, "So sad, such an ugly child." Her mother died of diptheria when she was 8; her father died of alcoholism when she was 9. By the age of 18, she was nearly six feet tall. Her voice was scratchy and her front teeth protruded—but she possessed enormous energy and a love for people.

When Franklin Roosevelt proposed, she accepted. When polio crippled him, it was Eleanor who told him he must be governor of New York.

He was elected, then won a race for the presidency. Later, Franklin fell in love with his secretary, Lucy Mercer. It was a relationship that lasted until his death. In fact, Lucy was with him at the end. When Eleanor heard of it, she wept briefly, then steadied herself. She had traveled 40,000 miles every year as a presidential representative because the handicapped president could seldom tour the country. In her absence, the president's relationship with his secretary had grown.

Wounded by her mother, her father, and her husband, Eleanor embraced all of humanity, especially the suffering. She reared her family and wrote 15 books. Year after year she was voted the woman most admired by American women.

When Eleanor died at the age of 74, Adlai Stevenson said, "Her glow has warmed the world." The United Nations stood in silence in her honor. Three presidents who had followed her husband stood with bowed heads as her coffin was placed next to her husband's in Hyde Park. Her motto had been, "Back of tranquility lies always conquered unhappiness."

In those words Eleanor Roosevelt offered martyred wives the key to victorious living. If you are a martyr, don't act like one! The Bible says when you fast, when you do without, don't let anyone know. Wash your face, be happy and God will honor you for it. A paraphrased version of Matthew 6:16,17 says, *"When you fast...don't do it publicly, as the hypocrites do, who try to look wan and disheveled so people will feel sorry for them...But when you fast, put on festive clothing, so that none will suspect you are hungry, except your Father who knows every secret. And he will reward you"* (TLB).

Betty Malz, who wrote *My Glimpse of Eternity* (mentioned in Chapter Seven), said, "I had to die to learn how to live." As a public speaker she has talked to thousands of women and is acquainted with their problems. She continues, "The one thing I tell wives whose husbands do not go to church with them is that they should be as attractive as possible and fill their homes with joy. Nobody is going to buy anything from a dowdy or depressed wife. As for eliciting sympathy from other Christians over your plight, forget it! They have their own problems. Laugh and the world laughs with you; cry and you cry alone. Perhaps your husband will never go to church with you, but don't plan on that basis. If you've lived your best, you may get a special crown. You can't lose! Heaven will be worth it. I know, because I've been to heaven."

I heard recently about a wonderful Christian woman who is married to a man who is a good husband in every way except one. He refuses to go to church with her. She has been a good wife and has reared their two sons to attend church. In fact, both of the boys went to Bible college and became ordained ministers. When they preach in the local church, their father refuses to attend.

This wife has been burdened for her husband for years. *Back of the tranquility that made her experience with the Lord so attractive to her sons lies conquered unhappiness.* She is active in the church visitation program. Her husband has never hindered her and she has not nagged him. Instead, she has concentrated on her strengths and committed her husband to the Lord.

In being cheerful and active and rearing their boys for the Lord, she has increased the possibility of her husband eventually being part of church life. Had she pouted, nagged, or acted depressed, she would have forfeited the satisfaction of working for God or seeing her sons go into the ministry.

As long as there is hope for your marriage, learn the secret of the golden zipper. What is the golden zipper? The term comes from those who have faced one-parent Christianity in a two-parent family and have found a key to the situation.

Treena Kerr, wife of Graham Kerr of "Galloping Gourmet" television fame, faced such a situation. Treena was the first in their family to become a born-again Christian. Christ delivered her from drugs, alcoholism and a disintegrating marriage. Soon afterward, she was given instructions on how to relate to her unsaved husband.

She was told, "Put a golden zipper on your mouth, keep no Bibles or religious books lying around the house. Don't nag, but pray." The Bible says, *"You wives, be submissive to your husbands, so that some, though they do not obey the word, may be won without a word by the behavior of their wives"* (1 Peter 3:1, *RSV*).

CHAPTER THIRTEEN

How You Can Experience the Ultimate of the Intimate Side of Marriage

The story is told of a middle-aged husband who went to his doctor and complained, "Doc, I am so worn out by the end of the day, I don't even have the strength to romance my wife." The doctor told him to jog ten miles a day for two weeks and then report back. Two weeks went by and the man phoned the doctor. The doctor asked, "Well, how are things going between you and your wife now?" The weary jogger replied, "Doc, I can't say, because I'm 140 miles away from home!"

Redbook magazine ran a survey of women's reactions to the question, "How satisfactory is your sex life?" The survey included several other questions—among them, "Are you a Christian?" When the responses were compared and grouped, it was discovered that Christian women had experienced the ultimate in intimate relations!

Playboy magazine ran a survey for men. This survey is interesting because *Playboy's* readers certainly would not be considered in the "hot-Gospel" category. People who responded were divided into four categories. On the one extreme were innovators who went in for sexual experimentation. Then there were less far-out types, the conventionalists followed by contemporaries and conservative traditionalists. Eighty-two percent of the men interviewed in this survey said they believed in a supreme being, and one-third of the men said they attended church regularly. The far-out innovators, those who believed in sex outside of marriage, were the least satisfied. The traditionalists, those who believed in the traditional concept of marriage, were the most satisfied by their sex life!

Don't let the devil tell you that playboys have more fun. They don't! You see, God designed sex. He told Adam and Eve to be fruitful and multiply. The Apostle Paul said, *"Marriage is honorable in all and the bed undefiled: but whoremongers and adulters God will judge"* (Hebrews 13:4). Sex is not a dirty word, but men have debased it to express something far below the purpose of God's creation.

Why do many committed Christians have the ultimate in intimate relationships? *Sex can be experienced on many levels*. Momentary satisfaction is all there is to the physical level. Beyond that is a relationship of two people who understand each other. That makes sex more meaningful.

Another plus is when two people are really in love and there is an emotional as well as an intellectual and physical oneness. That's even better.

But the ultimate in intimate relations is experienced when two people have a spiritual commitment to God and to each other plus all of the other things I have just mentioned. This culminates in total love and oneness.

Let me repeat, Christians *can* have the ultimate in intimate relations. That doesn't mean all Christians have attained the ultimate. The encouraging thing is that so many are working at it. Marabel Morgan, in her book, *The Total Woman*, has taken Christian sex out of the closet and helped people put some "zing" back into their marriages. She tells about the time she wanted to give her husband a pleasant surprise. She sent the children off to a relative, dressed up in her negligee; and when her husband came home from work, there she stood in all her glory. She said, "When he saw me, he dropped his suitcase, and he has never been the same since that time."

An Iowa farm wife tried the same thing on her husband. After being late, he burst in through the front door and said, "Woman, what are you doing, standing there dressed like that? The hogs are loose, and we've got to get them in!" I guess not everything works for everybody!

The Bible says that marriage is honorable. Like everything else, there is a danger that contemporary views of sex will color the biblical outlook of Christians. I heard of one Christian couple who went to X-rated movies for stimulation before having sex. I'd hate to think I had to look at an apple pie made by someone else before having a slice of apple pie made by my wife!

The Bible says, *"Know ye not that your bodies are the temple of the Holy Ghost?"* (1 Corinthians 6:19). The deepest satisfaction of sex comes with the knowledge that each partner is totally committed to the other and to God. A rehearsed technique cannot take the place of that deep assurance of love.

Most Christian couples can improve their sex lives by being aware of a problem. *The problem is this: most men emphasize sex and minimize tenderness; most women emphasize tenderness and minimize sex.* In fact, some women could almost live with tenderness and no sex.

If a man wants to improve his sex life, he should start with tenderness. If a woman feels her husband lacks tenderness, she should ask herself if she has responded adequately to her husband's attentions.

The quality of that important thing called sex in a marriage is determined by psychological factors as well as by physical factors. Psychological impotence can occur when a partner acts disinterested. The marriage may be headed for trouble if someone else acts interested in the frustrated mate.

The wife of a Hollywood star was asked if she didn't feel threatened by her husband's constant association with beautiful starlets. She said, "I take such good care of him at home that he really doesn't find the others attractive." There was a wise woman who realized what it took to hold her marriage together and acted accordingly.

I have never been able to figure out why a wife will spend three hours to shop for, cook and prepare a dinner to please her husband and not be smart enough to prepare a romantic evening in which love can be shared. If your husband is a little slow in this area, take the initiative. You may be amazed at the results!

I heard of a Christian family where the wife's needs were not met because her husband wrote poetry in every spare moment. When she engaged in a flirtation with a younger man who paid attention to her, she was harshly criticized. Actually, her husband's inattention contributed to her delinquency.

A pastor told me he was invited by a neighboring pastor to visit a man who was on the verge of a nervous breakdown. They approached an immaculate home and met a wife groomed to perfection. Then they met the husband, a gentle, attractive Christian man who had been totally rejected physically by his wife. This contributed to his problem. He had been a good husband in every way, and the home showed it.

The man's wife explained her attitude toward sex by saying, "Some people like watermelon and some don't." In all fairness, she should have told her husband she didn't like "watermelon" before they were married!

Then there was the wife who wrote me that her husband had intimate relations with her twice a year, once on Christmas and once on her birthday. He missed the point. *Lovemaking is the culmination of communication.*

What does lovemaking really mean to a man?

1. It satisfies his sex drive

A male has a continual sex drive, unaffected

by circumstances. It is hard for a wife to understand how her husband can be romantic after driving 400 miles a day on a vacation. What do you suppose he was thinking about for part of those 400 miles?

2. Lovemaking fulfills his manhood

A man's sex drive is linked directly to his ego. A wife's rejection in this area is interpreted in her husband's mind to mean, "I don't like you." He responds, "Then I don't like you, either!" Some feel they can hold on to their husbands with a clean house, good cooking and faithfulness. All of these attributes are good, but their effects will be nil if the men feel they have been *rejected as persons*.

Every so often I get a letter that tells of a husband who has left home after being married for years. The wife can't figure out what happened. Maybe he met someone who sent him a message of acceptance in the way she looked at him. I know it's wrong for a husband to be unfaithful to his wife—but his leaving, in most cases, could have been deterred.

Success in lovemaking can affect success in other areas of a man's life. The wife should be sensitive to his need. She should let him know she enjoys lovemaking. Many women have never let that be known. They look at sex as something

117

nasty people enjoy—that it's not nice. Their mothers told them, "Nice girls don't make love!" Since when? If nice mothers hadn't made love, there wouldn't be a human race.

3. Lovemaking enhances a man's love for his wife

When sex provides only gratification and is followed by guilt, it makes a mockery of what God intended to be a very satisfying experience. *It should be the ultimate expression of love.*

Sex should never be used as a reward. I know of one wife who could always get in the mood for lovemaking after a shopping trip. Most husbands can afford only so many of these rewards. A husband's lovemaking will never be enhanced if his wife looks on the performance as a duty. Passive cooperation is hardly an expression of love.

4. Lovemaking reduces friction in the home

A sexually-satisfied man is usually a contented man. Someone asked a man, "Do these women on the street ever bother you?" He replied, "No! Why should I look at a Volkswagen when I've got a Cadillac at home?"

What does lovemaking mean to a woman?

1. It fulfills her womanhood

If a woman considers herself unsuccessful in bed, she will have a difficult time accepting her womanhood. She has to feel needed or she will become insecure. A woman needs to feel that she fulfills her husband in every area of the marriage relationship or she will not be happy. For that reason she is especially sensitive to anything closely resembling criticism. If her husband even criticizes her cooking or anything else that has to do with her provision for his needs, she will react defensively. Men, criticism is not a "turn-on"!

2. Lovemaking reassures a wife of her husband's love

A woman needs love of all types, including companionship love. Few women enjoy solitude for long periods of time. Most men do not understand that a wife needs her husband's time.

Do you like to go places with your partner? Do you love to be together? This is how it was when you were first married. I have to be honest and say that my best friend is my wife. I like to have her with me all the time—about the only time she isn't with me is when I go hunting. Connie doesn't like to wade through the mud of a slough, hunting ducks. But she prays for me that I'll get something, and she gets up at five o'clock in the morning to make my lunch. That's pretty nice, right? And she puts little love notes in my lunch. That can certainly encourage a hunter! It even makes me anxious to get home!

You must spend time together to really be friends and stay in love with each other. The children feel secure when Mom and Dad are good friends. And when they're lovers, that's better yet!

I was preparing a sermon not long ago, sweating and working hard over my typewriter. My wife came over, threw her arms around me and gave me a great big kiss. One of my daughters ran into the other room and said, "They're at it again!" The kids just love it.

Husbands and wives have to be friends. A lot of people are looking for ultimate sex, but they never stop to realize that *ultimate sex starts with ultimate communication, ultimate understanding, ultimate acceptance, ultimate trust, ultimate love, ultimate touch—then ultimate sex!* This is how to experience the ultimate in your intimate relationship!

CHAPTER FOURTEEN

Heaven and You Can Make It Through

The devil is out to destroy your home! He has said, *"I will pursue, I will overtake, I will divide the spoil; my lust shall be satisfied upon them; I will draw my sword, my hand shall destroy them"* (Exodus 15:9).

It is the devil's business to divide and destroy homes. Why is this? In bringing conflict into a home, he can destroy the effectiveness of the believer's testimony and ministry.

Pat Boone is a well-known Christian. His daughter, Debby, in a newspaper article told how her parents fought bitterly in the late 1960s and how the family nearly broke up. Shirley Boone used to run outside to her car and drive off until things cooled down. On one occasion, Pat climbed on top of the car and wouldn't let her drive off.

Tragedy was averted. Debby said, "He realized he couldn't really compromise anymore and that he had to stay home more and devote his energy, time and love to us." Pat not only saved his home and lovely family—he saved his ministry as well.

What will it profit a man to save the whole world and lose his own children? Dr. Robert W. Smith, professor of philosophy at Bethel College in St. Paul, Minnesota, has touched the lives of hundreds of students. He and his wife have five children. He believes one of the first questions his Lord will ask him in heaven is, "Where are *your five?*"

Since the creation of man, Satan has leveled his attack on the home. Does it surprise you that Satan never approached Adam's wife until after their home was established? Does it surprise you that Satan did not approach Adam, the head of the human race, but Eve, his wife? Does it surprise you that the result of Adam and Eve's disobedience was loss of Paradise, loss of peace in the family and the murder of one son by his brother? These facts should not surprise you—

because the same attacks are being made upon families today with the same tragic results.

St. Augustine noted that woman was not taken out of man's head to challenge him, nor was she taken from his feet to be trodden down by him, but woman was taken from Adam's side where she could be close to his heart. This is God's plan for men and women today.

In so many marriages, the woman is either challenging her husband or being walked on. If couples would remember that the right relationship is to remain side by side there wouldn't be so many calling marriage quits.

Husband, don't leave your wife alone! She was meant to be by your side. When you fail to take her into your life, into your dreams, into your inner self, you leave her in a position where Satan can tempt her into wrongdoing.

The Bible says, *"And when the woman saw that the tree was good for food, and that it was pleasant to the eyes, and a tree to be desired to make one wise, she took of the fruit thereof, and did eat, and gave also unto her husband with her; and he did eat. And the eyes of them both were opened, and they knew they were naked; and they sewed fig leaves together, and made themselves aprons.*

"And they heard the voice of the Lord God walking in the garden in the cool of the day: And

Adam and his wife hid themselves from the presence of the Lord God amongst the trees of the garden. And the Lord God called unto Adam and said unto him, Where art thou? And he said, I heard thy voice in the garden, and I was afraid, because I was naked; and I hid myself. And he said, Who told thee that thou wast naked? Hast thou eaten of the tree, whereof I commanded thee that thou shouldest not eat?

"And the man said, The woman thou gavest to be with me, she gave me of the tree, and I did eat. And the Lord God said unto the woman, What is this that thou hast done? And the woman said, The serpent beguiled me, and I did eat" (Genesis 3:6-13).

Sin caused the first recorded argument in history! Adam blamed his wife, and his wife blamed the serpent. Instead of peace and harmony, there were tension, fear, insincerity and condemnation!

Sin brought two curses upon this first marriage. Because of sin, God said the husband would rule over the woman; and because of sin, the man would have to work, sweat, and die! (See Genesis 3:17-19).

These two judgments still hang over the heads of many today. Women often hate the dominance of men over their lives, and men hate their miserable, meaningless work. You can escape this curse upon life by accepting Christ's Lordship. The Apostle Paul wrote, *"For the law of the Spirit of life in Christ Jesus hath made me free from the law of sin and death"* (Romans 8:2). When Jesus Christ comes into a man's heart, that man is not going to rule over his wife as a merciless dictator. He is going to love her and cherish her as Adam loved Eve in the beginning. And his work will no longer be the sweaty futility it once was, but an expression of his love for the Lord and a way to relate to other people.

The way out of the curse upon life is to *recognize God's authority.* Like a magnetic force that pulls pieces of metal together, regardless of shape, God structures responsibility in a home. Without a higher authority, one person's opinion is as good as another's. It's like asking, "Which color is best?" Well, that's anybody's guess. But when you ask, "Which family pattern is best?" you'd better have an authority. That authority is the Word of God!

Paul writes that a spiritual leader must *"Rule well his own house, having his children in subjection with all gravity; for if a man know not how to rule his own house, how shall he take care of the church of God?"* (1 Timothy 3:4,5). "Rule" here means, "to stand before, to lead."

The husband is to give honor to his wife, and she is to obey and respect her husband. They are to be *"heirs together of the grace of life,"* and *"of one mind, having compassion one of another"* (See 1 Peter 3:7,8); and the children are to obey their parents (See Ephesians 6:1). Keep this structure clearly in mind and compare your own family situation to it. If it doesn't fit—change it!

Changing may take time. An ocean liner cannot make a sharp right-hand turn. You will have to recognize that habits in your home have built up a strong momentum. But start to change course, and God will bless you for taking action in obedience to His Word. Your first step should be to establish regular family devotions, then regular church attendance—mandatory, if you please. If the battle is to be won, it must be won in the home.

Several ministers gathered once a month, for nine months, to consider "the context of present-day youth problems." They listened to speakers representing different facets of society—a juvenile court judge, a psychiatrist, a school principal, etc. All said the same thing! The battle is won or lost in the home! The atmosphere of the home is more important than any other single factor in deciding which way young people will go, whether it is to heaven or hell!

Susannah Wesley faced an atmosphere in her home that could have been filled with despair. Half of her many children died, some with smallpox; debts mounted until credit was exhausted; and her husband went to jail because of these debts. The family had bread, but sometimes not much more. Her husband wrote, "All of this does not sink my wife's spirits."

Susannah was a frail woman, but she spent two hours a day in prayer and meditation and another six hours in her "household school." This continued for 20 years. Referring to her children, Isaac Taylor said, "There was not a one of them in which she did not instill a passion for learning and righteousness. She said, 'I will not raise children for the devil.'"

The choice you are taking is obvious. Your home will be a place of devotion or division, authority or anarchy, comaraderie or confusion, spirituality or sensuality. In the surveys we have conducted among Christians in the Midwest, only one in ten families has family devotions together. This is one reason why so many Christian families are having trouble, why so many churches lack the spirit of revival, and why so many pastors are discouraged because they see no spiritual progress in the families of the church.

The responsibility of family devotions rests upon Dad, who is to be the leader of the home. God said He knew Abraham would command his children after him. Dad, if you haven't been leading your family in spiritual matters, the best way to get started with family devotions is to confess your neglect to the family. Tonight at the dinner table, just tell your family, "I haven't been doing my part, and I'm sorry. As of today, we're going to begin reading the Bible and praying together as a family each day."

Set aside a regular time for family devotions

The most difficult thing about devotions is getting started. The children are not accustomed to the change and may grumble a little bit, but don't get discouraged. Your words may seem awkward at first; but after awhile, the family will look forward to the daily devotions. God can really work through their hearts in that time. In fact, it will prepare them for some of the problems they will face during the day.

Keep your devotions brief

Children have a short attention span, and they tire quickly unless the devotions move along rapidly. I often surprise the kids by ending the devotions before they expect me to. They will laugh and hug me because they know I am trying to be considerate.

Be honest with each other during your time together

Sometimes children think that devotions are times when their mom and dad use the Bible to preach at them. I've found that the way to erase this suspicion is to be honest with the family. When I come across a Scripture passage that speaks to my own weaknesses, I will confess my own sins and foibles to the family. It does something for the children when parents admit they aren't perfect!

Family worship will do many things for your home. *First, it will quiet your family down!* There is too much noise, too much bickering and arguing going on in many families. The realization that Christ is the unseen guest in your home will help everyone to still their outbursts of emotion.

Second, family devotions will teach tolerance and understanding. Many family problems can be eliminated by love and forgiveness. The Bible teaches the tender way of mercy, and mercy will help to heal the wounds of your family.

Third, family worship will cheer up your home! When your children realize that God is working in the family, they will be happy. It is great to have a goal you are *all* pulling for, and to know you will be together forever in eternity.

Fourth, family worship will teach moral values. America desperately needs spiritual guidance today. Young and old alike are asking what is right and what is wrong. The Bible is the great guidebook for moral decisions, and it will stabilize your family.

Fifth, family worship will strengthen you against suffering and sorrow. When you gather around God's Word and the presence of the Lord is near, God is able to minister by His Holy Spirit to the broken hearts in your family.

Another step in getting your spiritual priorities in order is to attend church together as a family

You might say, "Lowell, how do we choose the right church?" Well, just like people, churches have personalities. The personality of a church develops over a period of years.

Have you noticed that you identify with some people almost immediately? Others, no matter how hard you try, just do not offer the corresponding friendship and personality that meet your need. Sometimes this feeling is intuitive; you can't figure it out, but you just *know* there is a "kindred spirit" among certain individuals.

God has allowed variety in the types of churches that exist and also in the types of people that attend church. It used to be simple—there were just Catholic and Protestant churches. Protestant churches were divided into fundamentalist and nominal groups.

The fundamentalist churches placed great emphasis on the Bible, spiritual freedom and evangelism. Every other emphasis was called nominal (even though fundamentalist church hymnals were filled with hymns that owed their origins to "nominal" church backgrounds)! It was kind of simple and neat. The Catholic ducks swam in their pond; the Episcopalian ducks swam in their pond; the Methodist, Baptist, Assembly of God, Lutheran, and all other ducks swam in their own ponds.

Then something happened. God poured out His Holy Spirit, and now the ducks are swimming into one another's ponds! The one apparent common denominator is that God owns the ponds, and He raises the water level. Some ducks are still trying to stay in their exclusive ponds, but it is increasingly difficult for them to do so as the water level of the Holy Spirit gets higher.

With such a variety of groups confronting someone who is choosing a church, a few guidelines may be helpful. Two basic considerations are whether or not the church meets your family's needs and if your whole family feels at home in the church.

All denominations have some churches that are more spiritual than others. If you can find a spiritual church within your traditional denomination, good! *If not, then look around.* The spiritual future of your family depends upon your choice! If it is a choice between the spiritually dead "church your family always attended" and a spiritually alive church no one in your family has ever attended, opt for the spiritually alive church!

If, in the past, you always traded at a certain grocery store and then the prices went up and the food turned bad, would you have continued to trade there? If you always frequented a certain restaurant and then the quality of food and service declined, would you have still gone there to eat? I think you would have begun to shop around!

Sometimes people say, "I'm going to stay in my church and turn it around for God." In more than twenty years of evangelism, I have never seen that happen. I *have* seen countless people go to a dead church and lose out with God!

A little fellow was standing with his daddy in the foyer of a church. He noticed a plaque that said, "In Memory of Those Who Died In Service." He said, "Daddy, was that in the morning service or evening service?" If you are born again, find a "maternity" church where people are born again and where they are cared for. Don't attend a "cemetery" church where your enthusiasm for Christ is squelched.

Beyond that, *the spiritual needs of your family members are to be considered.* I know of parents who attended a church with just tolerable preaching, but they did so because the church youth program attracted their teen-agers. They decided, "We're going to make heaven, no matter what. It's the kids' spiritual lives we're concerned about."

Sometimes there are questions as to which church to attend. When in doubt, seek out the facts, check the endorsement of God's presence, and let the Holy Spirit guide you. You will feel an inner glow when you are worshiping at the right place, regardless of the size or status of the church! But whatever you do, *do it soon.*

Most problems reveal a spiritual need and require a spiritual solution. So let's talk about the solution—Jesus Christ. How is your personal relationship to Jesus Christ today? In facing your marriage problems, you are going to need help—His help. *And you will never stand taller than when you kneel in prayer.*

The ultimate answer to the question whether your marriage can be saved depends on your answer to another basic question, "Is Jesus your personal Savior?" Marriage manuals may give you guidelines, but the Bible offers you real answers to every area of your life.

If you have not received Christ as your personal Savior, do so now! He will forgive you as you confess your sins and trust in His death on the cross for your sinful past. It is like standing accused in court and hearing the judge say, "The penalty is $500 or three months in jail," and a friend in the courtroom offers to pay your fine. All you have to do is accept the provision—*and you're free!*

The Bible says, *"the wages of sin is death"* (Romans 6:23). Jesus offers His death for your payment. All you have to do is accept the provision.

Just pray this prayer: *Lord Jesus, I have sinned and failed You, but now I come to You and confess my sins and ask Your forgiveness. Thank You for paying the penalty for my sins on the cross. And, Jesus, now that You have saved me, help me to save our home and make it a wonderful place to be. Amen.*

Believe it. It's done! Now you have real hope. Paul said to the Philippian jailer, *"Believe on the Lord Jesus Christ and thou shalt be saved and thy house"* (Acts 16:31). Heaven's answer for your family is Christ in your heart and home, His Word and His love providing for every need of every member of your household.

CHAPTER FIFTEEN

Heaven's Motive for Your Marriage

More than a million marriages in the United States will fall apart this year. The experts have many explanations for this sad statistic. But one thing everyone seems to be agreed upon is this— it takes more than bread and a bed to hold a marriage together. Marriage partners need a worthwhile motive, a divine cause that binds them together and carries them over the rough places in their relationships.

Marriage was never designed to be a duet; it was created to be a trio. A husband and wife were meant to share their marriage with God. The reason so many marriages are failing is that God has been forgotten, except perhaps for the hour the family spends in church on Sunday mornings.

Another reason marriages are in trouble is couples expect more from marriage than people ever used to. Fifty years ago, men married women to help rear children, keep house and help carry on family traditions. Women married men who were honest and hard workers. All of this has changed. Today a man wants a wife, mistress, mother, adviser, wager earner, housekeeper and hostess, all in one woman. A woman wants a husband, lover, father, wage earner, friend and much more, all in one man.

During one of our Family Life Seminars, a man told me, "Lowell, it's tough to be the kind of husband a man has to be today." If you are not receiving what you desire from your marriage, it might be well to examine your expectations. You may be expecting more than your mate can deliver!

Your marriage should be a growing and nourishing experience. If you are looking for some excitement beyond your bedroom and kitchen, consider going into partnership with God. Someone has said, "If you want to live an exciting life, find out what God is doing and get right into the middle of it!"

At this very moment God is trying to build His Kingdom in your community. God is looking for men and women who will seek His Kingdom first, above all else. He wants families to express His will to the world.

This concept of partnership with God is missing in many Christian marriages. Somehow God is thought of as "the One who enhances our marriage" instead of as "the One we should serve." Too many people want fellowship without partnership.

The truth is, the primary reason for marriage is to serve God more effectively. The primary reason for rearing children is so they can grow up to serve the Lord. The primary reason for setting up a household is to create a visual expression of God's Family for your community to see.

I know these concepts might seem extreme; but as soon as you take God out of a marriage, you only have two bodies of flesh, and Jesus said, *"Watch and pray, that ye enter not into temptation: the spirit indeed is willing, but the flesh is weak"* (Matthew 26:41). Your flesh is too weak to hold your marriage together. You might have beautiful flesh, educated flesh, motivated flesh, powerful flesh—but it is still flesh, and flesh cannot satisfy the spiritual longing of your soul.

You see, deep within you is a desire to be part of God, part of His work here on earth. You need a divine motive for your existence as well as your marriage.

Look around! What is God trying to accomplish? He is trying to save as many from sin as He possibly can. God wants His children to grow and mature spiritually. He wants to reveal His might and power on behalf of those who need His help. And He is preparing Christians to inhabit His eternal Kingdom.

Now ask yourself, are you and your mate seeking His goals in your marriage? You may be professing Christians, but do you possess God's divine motive for your marriage? It is one thing to want to be *saved*, but it is another thing to want to *serve* God. It is one thing to *attend* church, but it is another thing to *build* His Church. It is one thing to *have religion*, but it is another thing to *be in partnership with God*.

If you want to enter into the most exciting and meaningful experience of your life, turn your marriage over to the Lord. Be certain that you have given your heart, soul, strength and mind to God as completely as you can. Don't worry about your mate. God will work in your partner's life. Just make certain that you belong entirely to God.

Then, instead of selfishly looking at your marriage, saying, "What am I getting out of this?" look for opportunities to serve God in your marriage.

Do these things for three months and see what happens!

Minister to yourself

When you wake up in the morning, turn your thoughts to God and express your love to Him. Pray before you get out of bed and it won't make much difference what happens after you get out.

One man told me, "Lowell, when I don't pray I can't get along with myself, to say nothing of getting along with my wife!"

Minister to your mate

Encourage your partner with praise. Your mate may be going through a personal struggle, and your words of faith will strengthen him and assure him of your love.

Husband, for you this will mean taking a moment to share a few tender moments with your wife. Hold her in your arms and assure her of your love and concern. Tell her you love her—in plain language. Remember, a man falls in love through his eyes, a woman through her ears. The more you say, the more your wife is assured of your love for her.

Wife, for you this will mean putting the "golden zipper" on your lips and obeying your husband. With the pressures upon men today, the last problem a man wants to have is a hassle with his wife. You can minister to your husband by supporting him with your love, prayers, and submission.

Minister to your children

If your children are in school, they are going to have to face the pressures of their own mental and social shortcomings. The teachers and curriculum are tough. It is hard to feel adequate when the tests show up so many shortcomings. Nonchristian classmates often ostracize dedicated Christians, and this makes it rough on every boy or girl who tries to live faithfully for Jesus Christ.

Help your children with their problems. Take time to talk. Show interest in their many frustrations as well as their accomplishments. Your children need your personal ministry.

Minister in your church

Chances are you will not end up behind the pulpit, but there are many positions in which you can serve God in your church. You can teach Sunday School, and in doing so, you will learn more about God's Word than ever before. If there isn't a Sunday School position open, volunteer your services to the pastor. But have your smelling salts ready—he might faint dead away!

Minister to your community

There are many community organizations in which you can express your Christian life. Kiwanis, Rotary, PTA and local political commitees are a few possibilities.

Minister to the nation

You can do this through the ministries God has raised that reach millions for Jesus Christ every week. These ministries are coming into your area by radio and television. Your faithful support will give you a personal ministry to the nation. I praise God for the partners who have stood behind the Lundstrom Ministries, enabling us to reach multitudes in moments through radio and television.

I need your help. If God is stirring you to do something for His Kingdom, write to me today. Tell me that you are standing with me and will help me with your prayerful support.

During the past several years of ministry, I have found that out of a hundred Christians who believe in a ministry, only one individual will support it. If you believe in this ministry, if I have been able to help you—then help me win others to Jesus Christ.

Minister to the world

You do this through your missionaries. As a family, it would be well if you adopted a missionary. Through the ministry of that servant of God, you would be ministering to another part of the world. When your family gathers around the table, you could pray for your representative. This step of faith and obedience to God's Word would give your family a special reason to exist.

Remember, the divine motive of your marriage is to *glorify God.* When you take His Kingdom to heart, God will bless your home. Jesus promised, *"Seek ye first the kingdom of God, and his righteousness; and all these things shall be added unto you"* (Matthew 6:33).

The lasting, meaningful things that you have searched for in your marriage will never be found outside of God. Get into the middle of what God is doing—with your family. It's exciting! It's fulfilling! It's lasting! Your heart will be filled with glory all the days of your life, and you will have Heaven's answer for your home.

If this book has been a help to you, please write and share your experience with me. You will receive a personal reply.

Lowell Lundstrom
Sisseton, South Dakota 57262

In Canada write:
Lowell Lundstrom
Box 4000
Winnipeg, Manitoba R3C 3W1